A SERIES OF LESSONS IN ISLAM

# Practices

FROM PRAYER TO PILGRIMAGE

Sayyid Ali Al-Hakeem

Author: Sayyid Ali Al-Hakeem

Translated and Edited by: The Mainstay Foundation

© 2015 The Mainstay Foundation

ALL RIGHTS RESERVED. No part of this work covered by the copyright may be reproduced or used in any form or by any means – graphic, electronic, or mechanical, including photocopying, recording, taping, web distribution, information storage and retrieval systems, or in any other manner – without the written permission of the Mainstay Foundation.

Printed in the United States.

ISBN: 978-1943393947

To our guide. To our hope. To our salvation.

To our Prophet (s).

# Contents

*About the Author* ............................................................................. *ix*
*Translator's Preface* ......................................................................... *xi*

    Introduction ............................................................................. 1
    Worship .................................................................................... 5
    Emulation ............................................................................... 13
    The Marjaeya ........................................................................ 25
    Knowledge ............................................................................. 33
    Islam's System of Worship ................................................. 45
    Prayer ...................................................................................... 55
    Reverence ............................................................................... 69
    The Mosque .......................................................................... 85
    The Holy Quran ................................................................... 97
    Supplication ........................................................................ 109
    Salawat ................................................................................. 117
    Fasting .................................................................................. 127
    Charity ................................................................................. 143
    Pilgrimage ........................................................................... 157
    Enjoining Good .................................................................. 165
    Modesty ............................................................................... 175
    Trade ..................................................................................... 191
    Remembrance of Imam Hussain (a) .............................. 203

*Bibliography* ................................................................................ *215*

# About the Author

Sayyid Ali Al-Hakeem is an esteemed Muslim scholar, lecturer, and researcher residing in Dubai, UAE. Sayyid Al-Hakeem spent ten years studying at the Islamic seminaries of Qum, Iran. There, he completed his Advanced Seminars (a Ph.D. equivalent in Islamic seminaries) in Islamic Jurisprudence and Thought. He also received a Master's degree in Islamic Thought from the Islamic University of Lebanon. Sayyid Al-Hakeem has dedicated the past twenty-two years of his life to service of the Muslim community in different capacities. He serves as a resident scholar in the Imam Hassan Mosque, Dubai. He is the Chair of the Religious Committee and the religious supervisor of the Charitable Deeds Committee of the Ja'afariya Endowment Charitable Council of Dubai.

# Translator's Preface

The task of translating Sayyid Ali Al-Hakeem's book was gratifying and enlightening. The book delivered precious nuggets of knowledge and polished pearls of wisdom in a style that is conversational and pleasant. This book is our attempt to pass these nuggets and pearls on to you in a style that is similarly conversational and pleasant. We thank the Sayyid for allowing us to benefit from this endeavor. We wish for him a life filled with scholarly attainment, in hopes that he will continue to pass along his treasures.

Here, we must humbly admit some of our biggest limitations. First, we must admit the great difficulty that comes with the attempting to translate the Holy Quran. Muslim scholars have pondered on the meanings of the holy text for centuries, and the meanings of its verses only grow deeper as time passes. The process of translation always begs us to find precise meanings for the passages that we translate. But when we encounter the majesty of the Holy Quran, we find ourselves incapable of understanding, let alone translating, its true and deep meanings. We turned to the works of translators who have attempted to do this before. Although no translation can do justice to the Holy Quran, we found that the translation of Ali Quri Qarai to be the most proper in understanding when compared to the understanding of the text as derived by our grand scholars. As such, we decided to rely on Qarai's translations throughout this book, with some adaptations that allowed us to weave the verses more properly with the rest of the work.

A second great limitation came with translation of the narrations of the Grand Prophet Muhammad (s) and his Holy Household (a). Their words are ever so deep and ever so powerful. We attempted to convey these passages to the reader in a tone that is understandable without deviating from the essence of the words of these immaculate personalities. We pray that we were successful in this endeavor.

Finally, we want to take this opportunity to thank you for your support. As students of Islam and as translators of this text, our greatest purpose is to please God by passing along these teachings to others. By picking up this book, you've lent your crucial support in this endeavor. We hope that you will continue your support throughout the rest of this book, and we ask that you keep us in prayers whenever you pick it up.

*The Editorial and Translation Team,*

The Mainstay Foundation

# Introduction

*In the name of God, the Compassionate, the Merciful*

Praise be to God, Lord of the Worlds. May God send His peace and blessings to the most noble of His creatures, the Holy Prophet Muhammad (s) and his Holy Progeny (a).

This book, *Practices: From Prayer to Pilgrimage*, is a compilation of fundamental lessons on rituals and practices in Islam. The book is meant to explain the philosophy and etiquette behind Islam's most important rituals. Along with chapters on prayer, fasting, and pilgrimage, the book looks at a number of other key practices, such as supplication and modesty. Finally, the book concludes with a chapter on the commemoration of the tragedy of Imam Hussain (a) as a form of devotion and commitment to God and His message.

The teachings of Islam have one unequivocal goal – to allow its followers to pursue excellence. From that perspective, Islam places great emphasis on knowledge and learning. We can see this clearly in the verses of the Holy Quran. These verses give knowledge a special status that is unique when compared with other human virtues. God says in the Holy Quran, *"Say, 'Are those who know equal to those who do not* know?' Only those who possess intellect take admonition."[1] God also says, "Only those of God's servants having knowledge fear Him."[2]

The traditions of the Holy Prophet (s) and his Progeny (a) contain numerous similar admonitions as well. It is narrated that Imam Al-Sadiq (a) said, *"The Messenger of God (s) once said, 'Seeking knowledge is an obligation on every Muslim. Verily, God loves the seekers of knowledge."* It is also narrated that the Commander of the Faithful Ali ibn Abi Talib (a) once said,

> *Oh people! Know that excellence in faith consists of seeking knowledge and acting in accordance to that knowledge. Indeed, seeking knowledge is a higher obligation for you than seeking sustenance. Your sustenance is pre-ordained and guaranteed. Your Just Lord has divided it amongst you and promised to deliver it to you. Surely, He will keep His promise. [On the other hand,] knowledge is protected by its keepers. You were commanded to seek it from its keepers, so go forth and seek it.*

Islam did not stop at admonitions and theories about knowledge and learning. Instead, it created opportunities and enabled conditions that would foster learning, research, and study. Amongst these was the establishment of Friday prayers – God says in the Quran, *"O you who have faith! When the call is made for prayer on Friday, hurry toward the remembrance of God, and leave all business. That is better for you, should you know."*[3] One of the important pillars of this ritual is its sermon, where the prayer leader must convey Islam's teachings, in

---

[1] The Holy Quran. Chapter 39 [Arabic: *Al-Zumar*]. Verse 9.
[2] The Holy Quran. Chapter 35 [Arabic: *Fatir*]. Verse 28.
[3] The Holy Quran. Chapter 62 [Friday; Arabic: *Al-Jumaa*]. Verse 9.

addition to addressing all other relevant worldly and otherworldly matters.

Dear reader, this series of books is based on a compilation of Friday sermons that I delivered over the years, as well as lectures I gave at a number of commemorations and celebrations. Throughout such gatherings, I have been able to address and speak on a wide array of issues relevant to the Muslim community.

At the insistence of a number of dear brothers, I compiled my notes to write these books with the hopes that God will accept the work and that the benefit will spread to the believers. I tried to maintain the conversational tone of the original sermons in order to make the books more reader friendly. After a series of these books were printed in the original Arabic, a group of believers then insisted to have the work translated into English so that English-speaking audiences may benefit as well.

I thank God, the Exalted, for His infinite support and favor. I must also thank everyone who participated in making this book a reality.

I ask God, the Almighty, to take this work as an act of devotion for His sake and to accept it by His grace, He is surely the All-Kind and Magnanimous.

Ali Al-Hakeem,

Dubai, United Arab Emirates

# WORSHIP

*In the Name of God the Beneficent the Merciful*

When we remember worship, we remember the man of excellence and distinction, the perfect human being, the one who God made as a protection and extension of the Message. The man that through his birth God answered the supplication of Prophet Ibrahim (a). *"When his Lord tested Abraham with certain words and he fulfilled them, He said, 'I am making you the Imam of mankind.' Said he, 'And from among my descendants?' He said, 'My pledge does not extend to the unjust.'"*[1] The Commander of the Faithful Imam Ali bin Abi Talib (a) – the legacy of God's prophets – was God's answer to Ibrahim's prayer.

It is not so simple to talk about the life of this immaculate individual. What speech, discussion, chapter or article can encompass the qualities and virtues of Ali bin Abi Talib (a)? Not only has this personality astounded the minds of generations, masses have been formed around his person. People are tried through him or by him, for he is the one who separates them between heaven and hell. Whoever followed him

---
[1] The Holy Quran. Chapter 2 [The Cow; Arabic: *Al-Baqara*]. Verse 124.

is destined to paradise, while those who opposed, fought, oppressed, and hated him are ordained to hell.

Imam Ali (a) was born in the holy month of Rajab which is the first month of the 3 holy months of worship and in the purest piece of Gods' earth. No other individual is popularly known to be the only human being to ever be born in God's House – the Ka'ba. Every day billions of Muslims face the Ka'ba during their prayers, submitting to God's will while their hearts gravitate towards it). Divine will had made this House of God the birth place of the Messenger's (s) successor and God's vicegerent. In this discussion of the significance of worship, we find it only natural to remember the worship of Ali (a) as the exemplar for mankind after the Holy Prophet (s). Though the mentioning of Ali (a) here will only reflect a drop of the ocean that is Ali (a), it will serve us well in understanding the importance of worship in our lives.

## Worship in Our Daily Lives

From the dawn of history until this day, humanity has not abandoned worship. Every society and all people cannot do without the dimension of worship in life. Indeed, one reason for this is that worship fulfills an innate calling to express ultimate devotion to the one upon whom a person's very existence relies. Although worship will differ from one person to another, as some worship God and others worship creation, we find that worship continues to be an undeniable theme. In worship there is usually absolute sanctification of the one that is worshipped. Worship manifests as a result of the realization of our innate nature regardless of whether people are drawn towards monotheism or polytheism. We further observe the significance of worship on a general level as it serves as a mechanism to fulfill our need to belong. More specifically, we discern the importance of worship in the lives of the believers as it serves in one's self-development and excellence.

## Worship and Belonging

When we are born we are innately drawn to analyze the world around us and realize that we are dependent. Being created is naturally connected to being dependent and having needs. Human beings naturally feel weakness, need and dependency; and thus, security is not realized unless we attain a sense of belonging. A person who belongs to something is one who feels strength in his presence because what he belongs to aids him in standing firm and treading through life's challenges. Without belonging, fear, hesitation and weakness slither back in when we are faced with the hardships of life. The need to belong is intrinsic to us. Our innate nature calls us to want to belong and attach to something of ability or power. One of the clearest examples of belonging is illustrated through worship. In worship, there is the submission of the dependent to the independent, the weak to the strong, the impoverished to the self-sufficient, and the servant to the master. This act of belonging could be practiced correctly and it could be carried out erroneously.

## The Incorrect Way

To worship and inadvertently belong to something that has relative power is the wrong path to take in worship. As human beings living in the material world we are attached, in a general sense, to material things. Wherever we turn we use our empirical senses and observe; and thus, we attribute power to the tangible things we see. Societies across history have worshipped a range of things they observed and attributed some force or power to. People have worshipped the sun, the moon, the sea, and other natural forces. Some societies that were characteristic of battle and war worshipped the god of war. Each community made attributions in accordance to what related to it and its observations. The fundamental mistake that all of these societies made is their lack of realization and acknowledgment of God's limitless power. This stems from the human attachment to the material world. From that you see human beings attributing partners to God with the hopes of fulfilling that belonging that he innately yearns for. Essentially, the innate nature of seeking to belong to the strongest absolute source of empowerment is sometimes hindered by the shortsightedness of feeling security from finite material things.

## The Correct Way

To worship and seek to belong with the absolute that is God is the correct path of worship. As human beings we have an innate nature that feels and acknowledges the existence of God and that God is the absolute power that gives us stability and security. The power and authority of God is unmatched; thus, worship comes in to further deepen this belonging to God etching his remembrance in the soul of the believer. The more a person is immersed in his worship of God the greater his attachment and loyalty is to Him. This is also accompanied by a greater sense of strength and ability because belonging to God means attaching one's self to the unlimited source of empowerment that gives existence to everything that is. The strength comes through sensing one's absolute weakness without God. The Commander of the Faithful (a) was the perfect exemplar of this belonging and attachment to God that came by way of worship. He saw a sign of God in everything and sought God in everything that he did. If we were to study the Imam's (a) life from its beginning to end we would observe the very same thing – complete immersion in the worship of God. His birth in the House of God (the Ka'ba) and his martyrdom in the House of God (the Mosque of Kufa) are just symbols of the strength of this belonging to God and his unwavering connection as His true servant.

## Worship and Striving for Excellence

*"I did not create the jinn and the humans except that they may worship Me."*[2] Service or worship of God is emphasized as a mechanism to increase one's knowledge and awareness of God. Knowing and being aware of God is the primary goal of creation according to our scholars. The way to achieve this knowledge and awareness is through the fulfilment of absolute worship of God. This is in addition to understanding and accepting that humanity was not created for this world to be its final destination; rather, human beings were created for an eternal afterlife. The more a person strives on

---

[2] The Holy Quran. Chapter 51 [Arabic: *Al-Dhariyat*]. Verse 56.

the path of excellence, the better fit he becomes to realize God's paradise. Excellence does not come except by way of sincere worship. Thus, the greater the worship and the more expansive the knowledge of God is; the better fit a person becomes to be the recipient of a lofty position with God. That is why you can observe that the prophets and vicegerents of God express pride and honor when they relay their attachment to God as His servants. Jesus (a) the son of Mary (a) proudly introduces himself when he says, "*Indeed I am a servant of God! He has given me the Book and made me a prophet.*"[3] The Commander of the Faithful (a) eloquently expresses this same honor, "*My Lord, it is enough honor for me that I am your servant and it is enough pride for me that you are my Lord.*"[4]

God gave virtue to his righteous servants and favored them over the rest of His creation in describing them by their state of worship. "*The servants of the All-beneficent are those who walk humbly on the earth, and when the ignorant address them, say, 'Peace!'*"[5] All of God's creations are under His rule, authority and will. In addition, all of God's creation can be called servants of God, as they are all utterly dependent on God, existing only within the realm of His absolute authority. However, the special designation here is a status of honor when God accepts a creation as His servant. The pinnacle of nobility, honor, and dignity is to be recognized by God as His servant, in its truest meaning as one who is completely obedient to Him and does not reject even His legislative

---

[3] The Holy Quran. Chapter 19 [Arabic: *Mariam*]. Verse 30.
[4] Al-Sadouq, *Al-Khisal*, 42.
[5] The Holy Quran. Chapter 25 [Arabic: *Al-Furqan*]. Verse 63.

will. All are bound by God's creational will, but creatures with free will can choose to disobey God's commands – His legislative will. If a creature's choices line up with God's legislative will, that creature can be nominated for the special designation as a servant of God.

History gives us a story that clearly embodies this understanding. There was a man at the time of Imam Moussa Al-Kadhim (a) by the name of Bishr Al-Hafee. Bishr was known to be of the people of affluence. He was keen to gatherings of entertainment, drinking, music and dancing. One day, Imam Al-Kadhim (a) was walking past Bishr's home. Out of Bishr's home came the sounds of forbidden song and music. The Imam (a) noticed one of the house servants throwing out the trash. The Imam (a) asked the servant a question – clarifying the significance of worshipping God – where he said: *"Is the owner of this home a free man or a slave?"* The servant replied, "Of course he is a free man." The Imam (a) responds, *"You're right. If he was a slave he would have obeyed his Master [God]."* The Imam (a) here so eloquently defined the meaning of worship and submission to God. If a person is to hold the title of 'servant' of God then he must be one who is obedient to Him – then and only then will he deserve that title. The house servant goes back into the house and finds her master Bishr at his table of intoxication. Bishr asks her why she has taken so long. She then notifies her master Bishr of the conversation she just had. Bishr jumps up and runs out of the house barefoot[6] searching for the Imam (a). He ran after the Imam (a)

---

[6] Because Bishr ran out to repent to Imam Al-Kadhim (a) with bare feet, he later became known as *Bishr Al-Hafee* (Bishr the Barefoot).

until he reached him. Bishr apologized and repented to God Almighty before the Imam (a).[7]

Bishr understood the words of the Imam (a), in that the honor of servitude to God is not deserved unless one is obedient to God. Bishr realized through the Imam (a) that the deeper one's worship of God is the closer he is to Him. God is the ultimate goal and worship is the staircase that we use to ascend to God. When we go back and remember the life of Imam Ali (a) we see a life full of such ascension. Worship filled the Imam's (a) time throughout his life, for he was always in a state of worship. How? Because everything he did was sincerely for God. He worshipped God in the sanctuary and in the battlefield, in caring for God's creation and in cultivating the land in seeking sustenance, in giving charity and in feeding the orphans and the poor. Ali (a) was the exemplar of the perfect human being, one that had attained the highest levels of worship and submission to God.

---

[7] Al-Hilli, *Minhaj al-Karamah*, 59.

# EMULATION

*In the Name of God the Beneficent the Merciful*

*Ask the People of the Reminder if you do not know.*[1]

One of the important issues that occupies a portion of many people's time and thinking is the issue of *Taqlid*, or emulation, in religious rulings. Is it obligatory or not? What is the proof for the necessity of emulation? Why emulate the most knowledgeable? There are many questions about this issue. We believe that everyone has a legitimate right to objective questions. This is especially true for the youth who stand at crossroads in their lives where different trends are attempting to attract them. Besides the purpose of addressing personal doubts one may have, the individual may find people that will debate him regarding his beliefs and his opinions. Therefore, it is important to form a complete and comprehensive vision so that we can walk our path with knowledge and insight. We encourage these questions as they show us that our community is alive; a community that thinks and reflects is alive and well; It is when the commu-

---

[1] The Holy Quran. Chapter 16 [The Bees; Arabic: *Al-Nahl*]. Verse 43.

nity stops thinking, reflecting, and questioning that we must begin to worry.

## WHY EMULATION?

There is an argument that is often repeated by some, though its meaning is not well thought out. They say that since the sources of religious rulings are clearly understood – the Quran is clear and our traditions are clear – there is no need to go back to the scholars for derivation of religious rulings. They argue that it's enough for a person to read the Quran and the narrations to understand what God wants from him.

This argument cannot be accepted because of the weakness of its premises. First of all, the Holy Quran is not readily understood for most people. The Quran has some verses that are summations while others are specific. Some of its verses are ambiguous while some are unambiguous. Some of its verses are absolute while others are restricted. Some of its verses are abrogating and others are abrogated. This makes it very difficult for a person to understand the meanings of the Holy Quran unless they have spent many years of their life seeking deeper knowledge of the Holy Book. In fact, the Muslims differed in their opinions and split into many sects due to their lack of knowledge in some of these matters and differences in exegesis. How can lay people, most of whom are not sufficiently versed in the Arabic language let alone the sciences of exegesis, claim to be able to readily understand the words of God?

The same is true for the traditions of the Holy Prophet (s) and his Household (a). There are narrations that are ambiguous and some that are unambiguous. Some are absolute and some are restricted. Some are trustworthy while others are weak. We also find some tradition reports that contradict – or seem to contradict – each other. A lay person who has not reached a sufficient level of scholarly knowledge will not be able to derive religious rulings from these sources.

With that said, there are two possibilities through which an individual can go about practicing his faith without going back to the scholars.

First, he can himself seek religious knowledge and become a scholar able to deduce the laws from their detailed sources. A person who has attained this high level of religious learning is called a *Mujtahid*, or jurist. However, the process of *Ijtihad*, or deduction of religious laws, cannot be undertaken by all of society. We cannot all enroll in a seminary and study for years to attain the level of jurist. Without diversity in occupations, societies cannot survive. Societies need physicians, lawyers, engineers, civil servants, etc. Without these diverse occupations, societal order cannot stand and the community will be paralyzed because it cannot fulfill some of its most basic needs. Therefore, we cannot expect the entire human race to dedicate their lives solely to the study of religion.

Second, a person can practice *Ihtiyat*, or precaution. This means that one must consider all possible rulings and take the safest option concerning every situation. Precaution in this way would ensure that the individual has a clear conscience in the eyes of God, as he has exhausted all possibilities in reaching what God truly wants of him. This is also a much more difficult route for a lay person to take. It requires knowledge of the rulings of more than one scholar; rather we must learn the opinions of the scholars from the beginning of the time of occultation to this day – all possible rulings based on the holy scripture. It requires that the person know the instances of difference between the scholars and how to determine which of the opinions is the most precautious. It also requires the individual to follow the most precautious ruling, which can indeed be a very difficult proposition for religious scholars, let alone lay people. Furthermore, sometimes precaution is not possible even for a religious scholar. For instance, if there is a possible opinion that the Friday prayer is forbidden during the time of occultation and there is another possible opinion that it is obligatory, there is no way to take precaution. One must then refer to the research of an expert jurist, or become an expert jurist himself.

## The Rationale for Emulation

We do not want to mention here the Quranic verses from which we deduce the permissibility of emulation. Nor do we want to mention the traditions of the Holy Household (a) that allow this, or the instances in which they instructed their companions to sit at mosques and answer believers' questions. There are tens of these texts in this regard. But analyzing these texts properly requires expertise that most people lack. In any case, such analysis is not required to justify the very basis of emulation. The road to emulation – referring to the research of experts – is one of common sense for most people.

The intellect pushes us to refer to those who know when we do not know. It is common sense that a person who does not have knowledge and expertise in a field should go back to the expert whenever he is in need of such skill. This is a rule upon which human societies are based. We cannot imagine any typical society, no matter how advanced or how simple, in which every individual has full and detailed knowledge that will address all aspects of life. There must be those who take physiology as their field of expertise so that we have doctors to go back to in times of illness. We need those who study engineering so that we can build habitable structures, roads, and bridges. But the engineer will need to refer back to the doctor when he is ill. And the doctor will need to go back to the engineer when he needs to construct a home. Each has knowledge and expertise in his field, but is ignorant when it comes to other fields. When individuals seek diverse occupations and fields of expertise, they begin to complement one another. They become interdependent. This means that interdependency in expertise is not just derived from sound reason, but is also a sociological phenomenon. Furthermore, this sociological phenomenon, this intellectual practice, has been under the close eye of the Prophet (s) and the Imams (a) throughout the ages. Their silent and vocal approval of this practice is a clear indication of its religious legality.

With all this said, it should suffice us to mention a few verses and narrations in this regard, without discussing them, as this is not the place for such a jurisprudential discussion.

God says in His Holy Book, "*Yet it is not for the faithful to go forth en masse. But why should not there a group from each of their sections go forth to become learned in religion, and to warn their people when they return to them, so that they may beware?"*[2] God also says, *"Ask the People of the Reminder if you do not know."*[3]

In a signed writing by Imam Mahdi (a), he wrote *"In your current affairs go back to the narrators of our traditions [i.e. the jurists], for they are my proof upon you and I am God's proof."*[4]

It is also narrated that when a contemporary of Imam Sadiq (a) asked him about whom he should ask if he had a question and could not reach the Imam (a), the Imam (a) said, *"You need only [ask] Al-Asdy."*[5]

These are amongst the tens of textual sources that our scholars look back to when discussing details on the issue of emulation.

## Emulating the Most Knowledgeable

After discussing the need for emulation, some may ask about the need for emulating the most knowledgeable scholar. Why can't we just emulate any one of the learned scholars? Why does it have to be the most learned scholar? Why do we have to refer to the most capable scholar in deducing Islamic law?

Referring to the most learned scholar is surely acceptable, and it is widely viewed as necessary. As for the legality of referring to another learned scholar when his opinion dif-

---

[2] The Holy Quran. Chapter 9 [The Repentance; Arabic: *Al-Tawba*]. Verse 122.
[3] The Holy Quran. Chapter 16 [The Bees; Arabic: *Al-Nahl*]. Verse 43.
[4] Al-Amili, *Wasael Al-Shia*, 18:103.
[5] Ibid. The Imam (a) referred the inquisitor to Al-Asdy, meaning Abu Basir, Yahya ibn Abi Al-Qasim Al-Asdy, a companion of Imam Baqir (a), Imam Sadiq (a), and Imam Kadhim (a).

fers from the most learned scholar's opinion, that is up for scholarly debate among the experts. Hence, the legality of referring to the most learned scholar is a given and is the option the non-expert should defer to in order to rationally clear his conscience before God Almighty. However, if the most learned scholar's expert research shows that it is permissible to follow another learned scholar, then that is a different story.

In the realm of expert research on this matter, some scholars have found that it is obligatory to go back to the most knowledgeable of scholars while others do not believe that it is an obligation. And the issue is not just a matter of debate for the scholars of the school of thought of the Holy Household of the Prophet (s); rather, other schools of thought of Islam have also debated this matter. Al-Ghazali, a renowned Sunni scholar, wrote,

> *And the most appropriate – seems to me – is to follow the best. Whoever believes that Al-Shafi'i, may God have mercy on his soul, is more knowledgeable and has a better probability of being right, he cannot take the school of thought of another based only on whim.*[6]

This is the line of thinking of most Shia scholars. There are some late scholars, such as Al-Sayyid Al-Murtadha, that have even claimed that it is so widely accepted that it is a given for Shia Muslims.

The most important proof in this regard is the standard of reason. The reasonable individual will take the opinion of

---

[6] Al-Hakim, *Al-Usool Al-'Aamma lil Fiqh Al-Muqarin*, 629. Citing: Al-Ghazali, *Al-Mustasfa*, 2:125.

the most knowledgeable expert, especially when something really significant is at stake. This is also evident as a practice in societies across the board. We see that when a more experienced, skilled, and knowledgeable expert is available to provide a service, we would prefer him over a less experienced and knowledgeable expert. If someone is given an option to choose between two doctors, one of whom is more skilled, he will doubtlessly choose the more skilled doctor, especially when his life is at stake. This is the case in any other art or science when something drastic is at stake. Similarly, when one's eternal afterlife is at stake, the reasonable necessity of referring to the most learned religious scholar becomes evident.

In other words, we can build the argument as follows. As mentioned earlier, referring to the most knowledgeable scholar will certainly clear your conscience in God's court of justice. The most knowledgeable jurist is either the only jurist whose emulation will suffice for you to fulfill your obligation, or he will be one of two or more jurists whose emulation will suffice in the same way. If we assume that it is obligatory to emulate the most knowledgeable, you must emulate him and no one else. If we assume that it is not obligatory to emulate the most knowledgeable, you have done no wrong by following him anyways. In either case, you have certainly fulfilled your duty towards your faith if you follow the most knowledgeable expert, whereas you have fallen in a position of doubt if you follow anyone else. Moreover, the expert scholars who maintain the necessity of emulating the most learned expert have not found the sufficient evidence from the Holy Scripture to justify allowing people to refer to other learned experts. Hence, referring to the most learned expert is the emulation option that clears a non-expert's conscience.

## Emulating a Deceased Scholar

Another of the important questions regarding emulation consists of the need to emulate a scholar who is alive and not being able to emulate a deceased scholar. Why is this the case? Does the knowledge of the scholar dissipate after his death, such that I cannot refer back to his books any longer? If the scholar that I follow now passed away, must I refer back to some other scholar and begin learning the rules of my religion all over again based on his opinions?

We cannot give a thorough jurisprudential answer to this question here because this, again, is an issue of debate between our scholars. Some of our scholars' research concludes that one is allowed to emulate a deceased scholar initially, while others' research concludes that one is allowed to continue to emulate him only if one began emulating him during his lifetime. Each scholar has his own opinion based on his jurisprudential principles and understanding of the texts.

For non-experts, what we can say in this regard is that the expert scholars we are allowed to follow are either both the living and the deceased or only the living. Hence, when one considers this on its own merit, following the expert research of the living scholar is sure to clear the individual's conscience in the Divine court of justice, while following the deceased is up for debate. The evidence at the very least allows us to refer to the living scholar, but there is question on whether or not it allows us to refer to the deceased scholar initially. Therefore, we can only reasonably rely on what is proven to relieve us of our responsibility, and that is to refer to a living expert jurist. That way our conscience is clear and we have surely fulfilled the bare minimum of our responsibility. Coupling this with the fact that we must refer back to the most knowledgeable scholar, as described earlier, we conclude that the sound course of action for a non-expert is to refer to the most knowledgeable scholar among the living scholars.

At times, the most knowledgeable of the living jurists may have the expert opinion that a person can continue to refer to the opinions of the deceased scholar which one had followed while that jurist was alive. In such a situation, we are primarily following the most knowledgeable of the living scholars and it is only by his expert opinion that we can continue in our emulation of the deceased scholar (all according to the conditions and regulations stipulated in that living scholar's research).

As for the expert jurist debate on this matter, it requires that one delve into a thorough analysis of the holy scripture. But the non-expert generally does not have the prerequisites for such a discussion. Moreover, since the reasonable default is to refer to the most knowledgeable living scholar, the non-expert need not delve into the matter further.

It is important to contemplate on the reasonable default in referring to the most knowledgeable living scholar. This requirement fosters renewed scholarship throughout the ages. It makes it very difficult for there to be intellectual stagnation. Within the Twelver Shi'ah Muslim School, in the age of occultation, the doors of *ijtihad* (expert deduction) are wide open. There is continuous refinement of jurisprudential principles and evolving skill in applying the deduced laws to fit the needs of the time.

It is true that the expert scholars may differ in their conclusions. Indeed, the occultation of the Twelfth living Imam (a) deprives us of direct access to the right answers on several questions. But God Almighty wants us to have the right answers and the Imam (a) wants us to have the right answers as well. Hence, the occultation must have been because of some barrier resulting from humanity's exercise of free will. There may be other wisdoms behind the occultation, which will become known upon the reappearance of the Imam (a).

But what are we to do when our Immaculate Imam (a) is in occultation? The next best option that we have after a guaranteed correct answer – an immaculate answer – is an expertly deduced answer. We have nothing but the apparent commands that upright, expert scholars are able to objectively deduce from the sources. These scholars sift through the sources, attempting to filter out fabricated traditions, struggling to understand the true commands of God that our Imams (a) communicated. These apparent commands may in fact be the real commands in many cases, but in some cases they may not be (albeit unknowingly so). That is despite the great efforts that our jurists put into deriving them. In either case, following this expert research is an option that God Almighty allows, given the circumstances. If and when we realize the great effort that the expert jurists put into deriving even a single ruling and the dedication that they have for daily learning and teaching, we would know that the issue is not an issue of personal whims and ulterior motives. The process of deducing these rulings is delicate, serious, and strenuous. The upright, expert jurists do this out of sincerity and dedication to the Twelfth Imam (a). The lives of intellectual rigor and asceticism they lead are far from a craving for power and authority over this short, fading life, as some may allege.

# The Marjaeya

*In the Name of God the Beneficent the Merciful*

*We sent down the Torah containing guidance and light. The prophets, who had submitted, judged by it for the Jews, and so did the rabbis and the scribes, as they were charged to preserve the Book of God and were witnesses to it. So do not fear the people, but fear Me, and do not sell My signs for a paltry gain. Those who do not judge by what God has sent down—it is they who are the faithless.*[1]

The discussion on the necessity of establishing a connection and strengthening the relationship with Imam Mahdi (a) such that it changes from being a theoretical and conceptual relationship to a practical relationship – a relationship in which we are able to give and take, and moreover, feel his presence and understand the blessings that emanate from him – is of significant importance. One of the means of connecting with Imam Mahdi (a) is through connecting with his representatives and the carriers of his grandfather's message (protectors of the Book). Here, we are not in a position to expand the discussion on the status of scholars and ex-

---

[1] The Holy Quran. Chapter 5 [The Spread; Arabic: *Al-Maeda*]. Verse 44.

plore how to connect with them, how to consecrate them, how to respect them, and how to benefit from them. This is a lengthy topic that requires a separate discussion. What concerns our discussion is the connection with the scholars and jurists because they are the representatives of the Immaculate Imam (a). We will focus on a number of points.

## Referring Back to the Scholars and Jurists

One of the important pillars that the Ahlulbayt School of thought and the continuation of Ahlulbayt's message is built on is the emulation of the carriers of their narrations - the students of their school and the jurists deriving the jurisprudential rulings from their traditions. This is the most important issue amongst all the issues in establishing the practical connection with Imam Mahdi (a). Our obligation is to follow all that God the Almighty legislated and to refrain from that which He forbade. People came to know and understand what God legislated and forbade by asking the Prophet (s) during his life.

When the believer would need to inquire into a religious ruling, he would ask the Prophet (s) directly. The Prophet's (s) answer would be the religious ruling that reflects what God requires from the person. After the demise of the Prophet (s), the school of thought of Ahlulbayt believes that the Imams (a) are the relaters of the rulings, and their say is that of their grandfather the Messenger of God. When a believer needed to inquire into a religious ruling, he would ask the Immaculate Imam. The Imam would answer him and convey the religious ruling. This ruling would necessarily be true because we believe in their Immaculateness.

However, during the time where we cannot reach the Immaculate Imam directly, like our contemporary time, how is it possible for the religiously liable one to know the religious ruling? How can one fulfill his religious obligation with certainty? The religiously liable person certainly knows that he is commanded to do many things and asked to refrain from numerous others. However, he is not able to know in great detail all of these religious rulings. What should he do? What is the obligation? We attempted to answer these questions in the previous chapter when we referred to the notions of: becoming an expert jurist, taking precaution, or emulating an expert jurist.

## Emulation is Connecting with the Imam (a)

### The Jurist is a Means to Connect with the Imam

Emulation must be viewed as one of the key factors in committing to the orders of Imam Mahdi (a), may God hasten his reappearance, such that it is one of the avenues in connecting with him (a). The individual must view the jurists, through his connection with them, as the representatives of the Imam (a) and understand his relationship with them through that lens. In essence, the primary relationship is with the Imam (a) and then secondarily with the jurists.

### Rejecting the False Claimants of this Position

The institution of Marjaeya (the religious authority of the jurists) holds a high status and is highly revered and respected by the Followers of Ahlulbayt (a). This is due to the sacred knowledge the jurists carry and the piety they possess. However, this status and reverence from people draws some people who have ill souls and intentions to claim this grand status with a desire to gain materialistically. This is common as history has taught us of people who have claimed higher positions such as that of Imamate, Prophethood and even Lordship. For that reason the believer must be advised as they must be cautious of people that claim these positions wrongfully and must not be influenced by propaganda that is advanced by these claimants. It is imperative to verify the validity of the claims made by those claiming these positions and not to accept simply anyone claiming Marjaeya. Some, due to their religiosity and trusting outlook of those who wear the turbans, do not doubt turbans that claim this lofty status. Thus, they shy away from standing in their way since they are scholars and it is inappropriate to address them in an improper manner.

We are not advocating confrontation with others, even though this might be necessary when one is dealing with hypocrites who try to exploit people who are religious and kindhearted. However, what we are advocating for is to take caution and demonstrate diligence by refusing to simply accept anyone claiming the position of Marjaeya. We have to go back to the religious guidelines and confirm the validity of such claims. It is not permissible to accept simply anyone who claims to be from the jurists as one of the jurists. Rather, we should only accept those who we verify have fulfilled all the conditions for emulation that are specified in the books of jurisprudence.

## Diversity in Religious Leadership

It is natural to have diversity in the Marjaeya as a religious leadership because Marjaeya is not like Imamate where the

Imam is appointed by the designation of the preceding Imam or Prophet. The religious leader of the institution of Marjaeya is identified when certain defined conditions are present in a person. This naturally results in having more than one qualified jurist and creates diversity within the institution of religious leadership. A person can emulate a particular jurist because he finds that this person is qualified according to the religious guidelines and criteria while another individual might refer to another jurist because he finds that such a jurist is qualified according to the religious guidelines and criteria. This does not necessitate that one who emulates a particular jurist must not recognize the legitimacy and qualification of others. Emulating a jurist is not of the same nature as following a certain faith or political party. The relationship with the jurist is built on faith and referring to him for religious rulings. It does not require that he should be supporting him against others. Rather, we should all respect our jurists who meet the conditions and are qualified to assume this religious leadership. Emulating one of them does not eliminate the others in respect to their knowledge or religiosity. We must embrace those jurists' positions and status and treat them with respect and admiration because of what they carry from the heritage of the Great Prophet (s) and his Holy Household (a), and the religiosity and piety they possess.

*Religious Criteria of Emulation*

What is especially important for the Followers of Ahlulbayt is that they pay significant attention to the religious guidelines and criteria. The Imams (a) stressed this point with their followers such that it became a prevalent characteristic in them over time. Perhaps one of the reasons why this small minority was able to protect itself despite the hardships that it faced is its commitment to the religious guidelines and standards. They do not follow any leader blindly and are not lured by resonating slogans. Rather, we find them concerned with the religious standards. From this aspect we find that the issue of Marjaeya, in general, is not subject to marketing or propaganda or promoted in order to support particular groups. Rather, it is subject to the religious standards determined through knowledge and piety, and other relevant conditions that must be present in the jurist. Unfortunately, it is noticeable that there are some calls advocating for emulation based on irrelevant considerations that are not related to the strictly religious standards.

Some propose to emulate some jurists because their rulings are easy, they are more knowledgeable than others in matters irrelevant to the position of religious authority, they have good presence in the media, and based on other criteria that are irrelevant to religious authority.

These irresponsible or irrelevant considerations do not amount to essential conditions necessary in a qualified jurist. Indeed, such whimsical standards are neither supported by sound rationale nor the narrations of Ahlulbayt (a). Even if one were to entertain the notion that some of these proposed considerations have arguable relevance, the difficulty then lies in outlining the objective criteria for identifying the jurist with such qualifications. This important matter must not be left up to personal interests, emotional influence, and subjective preferences. For, indeed, all such tendencies are far from the religious standards and guidelines which the

Imams (a) have outlined for us in order to facilitate the selection of a jurist that must be emulated and referred to for religious rulings.

If adhering to the religious guidelines and criteria is important in all matters, it would be of paramount importance in the issue of emulation. That is because much of a person's religious practices require proper emulation. A typical believer's faith depends on it. A person must be more protective of his faith than of his money and children, or anything else of value. Religion is one's ticket to eternal salvation and is thus more valuable than anything else. It is unreasonable and forbidden for one to abandon his religion in order to serve the worldly interests of others. That would make him the worse of people as is narrated by the Commander of the Faithful (a), *"The worst of people is that who sells his religion for others' [worldly pleasure]."*[2]

The religious guidelines require us to refer to the most qualified jurist when the jurists have different opinions. But how can we determine who the most knowledgeable jurist is? Furthermore, in certain cases, we may also need to know which jurist takes the most precaution when issuing verdicts. How do we know who that is exactly? Who will help us in making this judgment? The answer lies in referring to a particular group of specialists. These are the high-ranking scholars and advanced-level teachers in the Islamic seminaries who are renowned and established in their scholarly activity. Such experts who have examined the research of the various jurists can easily help us identity the most knowledgeable or most precautious jurist. We can either take the

---

[2] Al-Wasiti, *'Uyoon Al-Hikam wa Al-Mawa'ez*, 117.

reasonable route by referring to the experts in this field and asking for their opinion, or we can take the risk of a lifetime and an afterlife by following our own desires if we choose the scholar for simply having the seemingly 'most lenient' or so-called 'progressive' rulings.

# Knowledge

*In the Name of God the Beneficent the Merciful*

*Say, 'Are those who know equal to those who do not know?' Only those who possess intellect take admonition.*[1]

Human beings are unique relative to the rest of God's creation in that they are not only living but they have the faculties of intellect and reason. These faculties are what actually gave humanity the distinction of being chosen as the leaders of the world. Unlike animals, human beings are able to think abstractly, theorize, conceptualize and utilize their intellect and reason to advance themselves. Thus, as the religion of God that realizes this reality, Islam calls its believers to seek knowledge. God has made the measures of sophistication and greatness directly related to knowledge. In the eyes of Muslims, seeking of knowledge is linked to their belief in God as opposed to the philosophies of other faiths that fought and ostracized the scientists of their communities. In those communities, they considered any scientific innovation to be heretical which pushed the scientists, thinkers and reformers to form ideologies and strong

---

[1] The Holy Quran. Chapter 39 [Arabic: *Al-Zumar*]. Verse 9.

movements that separated completely between religion and science. On the other hand, we see that knowledge and science grew in the arms of Islam. With the advent of Islam, people that were once in the shadows of ignorance transformed toward the light of knowledge, and within years the Muslims became the greatest civilization that history has witnessed. That was all due to the grace of religion and its teachings that called people to seek knowledge and focus on all types of sciences. By that, the status of humanity would be advanced and humanity could afford further services.

Shedding light on some of the issues that are linked to the subject of seeking knowledge and the necessity of benefiting from every moment will add to and diversify our already existent knowledgebase. Some of the significant elements of this discussion include:

1. The Necessity of Seeking Knowledge
2. The Significance of Linking Knowledge to God
3. Not Being Complacent with Academic Curricula
4. Our Perspective on Teachers

## SEEKING KNOWLEDGE

Our era has seen great technological advancement and scientific breakthroughs in science. With all of the criticisms and negativities that may have come with the different scientific theories and ideologies that have come forth, it is important not to forget the following fact: we are all capable, in one way or another, of seeking knowledge and of choosing any of the different fields of science to study. The institutions that were built in developed countries have provided this opportunity. It very well could be one of the great blessings of God that our countries' materialistic advancements in business and wealth have opened the doors of opportunity for the growth of education and science. Within a matter of a few simple years, we have witnessed societies transform from ignorance and illiteracy to education and progress.

Seeking knowledge was probably one of the hardest tasks and endeavors. People would put forth all their effort and savings just to get an education. Some would travel to different countries across the globe in pursuit of knowledge and education. Others would struggle between jobs and continue to pursue education. These examples still exist today; however, there is much more ease than before in getting an education and seeking knowledge. Books are readily available in print and online, learning resources are found in various platforms including the web, and the means to education are generally much easier than they were in the past. Therefore, there is no excuse for not seeking knowledge and education to escape the darkness of ignorance.

In addition, we are able to improve our standing as individuals and realize our humanity through seeking knowledge. It is narrated that the Holy Prophet (s) said, "*The people with the greatest value are those with the greatest knowledge, and the people with the least value are those with the least knowledge.*"[2] Imam Ali (a) also said, "*The value of every man is in what [he knows].*"[3] Thus, we must take advantage of the opportunities before us and not be heedless of God's blessings. We are fortunate to have so many opportunities that many people in other

---

[2] Al-Reyshahri, *Mizan Al-Hikma*, 3:2066. Citing: Al-Sadouq, *Al-Amali*, 73.
[3] Ibid. Citing: Al-Sadouq, *Al-Amali*, 532.

countries are not privileged to. However, we should not be ones who seek an education simply to secure a job or some type of position. Do not sell yourself short by doing that; rather, immerse yourself in seeking knowledge because it is your greatest tool in facing the challenges of life.

## Linking Knowledge to God

On the importance of knowledge as one of the greatest blessings of God, Al-Shaheed Al-Thani, may God be pleased with him, said:

> *Know that God made knowledge to be the holistic factor in the design of the highness and lowness of this world… God said in the Holy Quran, 'It is God who has created seven heavens, and of the earth [a number] similar to them. The command gradually descends through them, that you may know that God has power over all things, and that God comprehends all things in knowledge.'[4] This verse is enough evidence to illustrate the honor of knowledge, especially the knowledge of the oneness of God. The study of God's oneness is the foundation of every science and the center of all knowledge. God made knowledge the highest and most noble and the first element of strength that Adam was given after his creation, to leave the shadows of absence to the light of existence. God said in the first chapter that he sent to His Prophet Muhammad (s), 'Read in the name of your Lord Who created; created man from a clinging mass. Read, and your Lord is the Most Generous, Who*

---

[4] The Holy Quran. Chapter 65 [Divorce; Arabic: *Al-Talaq*]. Verse 12.

taught by the pen, taught man what he did not know."[5] *So ponder on the opening of the noble, honorable, holy book that does not give falsehood to anyone who holds it... the revelation came from the Wise and Praised with the blessing of creation and reinforced it with the blessing of knowledge. If there was a strength to reinforce humanity with after its creation that is greater than knowledge, God would have given it just that...*[6]

Knowledge is so significant for us in God's eyes. It is the greatest strength for us after our creation and existence. If we can connect our knowledge to God Almighty, we can reap the benefits of knowledge much more readily. There are many benefits from this that we can observe in our lives:

*Seeking Knowledge as Worship*

When a person connects his search for knowledge to God, he will receive all the rewards and benefits that God has ordained for those who seek knowledge. The number of narrations that discuss the great reward of knowledge seekers is vast. These narrations illustrate that if the knowledge seeker's intention is in pursuit of God, then he is guaranteed ample rewards; however, if his intention is simply the pursuit of this world, whether it's getting a degree, a job or a promotion, he will get only that.

It is narrated that Imam Al-Sadiq (a) said, "*Whoever learned for the sake of God, worked for the sake of God, and taught for the sake of God, he will be known in the kingdom of the heavens for greatness*

---

[5] The Holy Quran. Chapter 96 [The Clot; Arabic: *Al-'Alaq*]. Verses 1-5.
[6] Al-Shaheed Al-Thani, *Munyat Al-Mureed*, 93.

*and it will be said that he learned and taught for the sake of God."*[7] It is unfortunate that we sometimes raise our children to see school as a necessary evil from day one. Also, we tend to emphasize that the benefit of getting education is that it is the way to receive a degree that will make one more marketable in securing work to make a living. Education becomes a living nightmare for sixteen or more years until the young man or young lady finally graduates with their degree and gets a salaried job. In this demeanor, a person wastes the best years of his life for something that is only temporal. However, raising our children with a culture that enfranchises them to seek knowledge because it is what will elevate them with God will produce a more promising outcome. We need to teach our children that learning, getting an education, and seeking knowledge is something that God loves. When we educate ourselves we are pleasing God. If our intention is to please God, even if we do receive degrees to get jobs and make a living, our pursuit can still be linked to God and serving Him. Our intentions should be sincere that in getting the position we sought we will be using such a position to serve His will and do God's work on Earth. With our jobs and positions, earned after education, we can serve our people and our nation that nurtured us. Moreover, it is vital to see that God is the end and everything else is a means to reaching that end.

If education were built on this foundation, things would be very different than they are now. Today many people's primary goal in getting an education is simply to make a living via the degree. So, a common result is pursuing the degree

---

[7] Al-Reyshahri, *Mizan Al-Hikma*, 3:2087. Citing: Al-Tusi, *Al-Amali*, 47.

without much attention to one's quality in learning so long as the degree is received. Pursuing education, with God in mind, differs greatly especially in regards to the time, effort, and quality of learning.

*Knowledge and Ethics*

When education is linked to God, its effects will be positively reflected in a person's ethics and spirituality. Without that connection those areas will be affected negatively. A scholar who has sought knowledge for the sake of God is humble, because the more he knows the more he realizes how little he knows and how the little that he knows is completely dependent on God Almighty. He acknowledges the greatness of God, His knowledge, and His dominion; and thus, the scholar increases in humility and humbleness before God. People without God in mind become more arrogant and conceited when they increase in their knowledge, because knowledge to them is only an instrument to gain in this world. The person whose ambition is limited to this world is of lowly aspiration. This truth is clarified in the following narration from the Holy Prophet (s):

> *Whoever sought knowledge for the sake of God, he would not [learn a piece of wisdom] except that it increases his humility, compounds his humbleness among others, intensifies his fear of God, and multiplies his exertion for the sake of his faith. He is the one who benefits from knowledge, so let him gain knowledge. And whoever sought knowledge in pursuit of this world, status with people, and to gain favor with those in authority, he would not [learn a piece of wisdom] except that it increases his arrogance, he transgresses against people, he becomes conceited and grows further away*

*from religion. He is the one who will not benefit from knowledge, so let him stop and not strengthen the case against himself. [Let him stop and avoid] the regret and shame on the Day of Judgment.*[8]

*Knowledge's Blessings*

There are secondary effects that arise from seeking knowledge for the sake of God: the blessings of goodness. God has the keys to everything, as he is the master and owner of everything; thus, when a person embarks on the journey of seeking knowledge, God will open every closed door for him. Parables of ancient scholars tell us that whenever they were in a bind of figuring out a certain issue they would direct themselves to God in prayer and supplication. Thereafter, those closed doors would open up for them and the issues they couldn't resolve were simplified. On the other hand, those who sought knowledge without God in mind were stripped from such blessings. It is narrated that the Holy Prophet (s) said, *"Whoever learned knowledge to show off [, in duplicity,] seeking this world, God strips away his blessings and restricts his livelihood..."*[9]

## COMPLACENCY WITH ACADEMIC CURRICULA

Much of academic curricula, particularly in primary education, have been based on surveying topics instead of providing depth to certain areas of study. Schools provide students a great amount of information on a number of subjects so that students can specialize in the area the student desires

---

[8] Al-Reyshahri, *Mizan Al-Hikma*, 3:2079.
[9] Al-Majlisi, *Bihar Al-Anwar*, 74:100.

later on in the future. School curriculum in such cases is based on the rule of "a rose from every garden," whereby the school will give the student something from every field so that he may build on that minimal foundation later on. Thus, a student should not be complacent and stop at what his primary education offers him. Rather, he should benefit from the keys that his schooling has given him to open doors that will deepen his knowledge.

Some schooling methods have generally relied on feeding the students with information to commit to memory, whereby the student is given information as scientific fact and is taught what have been believed to be correct theories in every science at some point in time. Thus, he is bound to take such information as mere fact regardless if the information is actually accurate or has been based on old theories that have already become outdated. In many of these cases of schooling, the student is not encouraged or even allowed to debate or object to the information at hand. On the other hand, there are other methods of schooling which focus on expanding the student's mind rather than just feeding him information. For instance, this occurs by helping the students notice patterns, draw conclusions from examples and by the use of analogies. There are differing opinions on which method is more beneficial for students in their primary schooling, and that argument is not something I wish to delve in here; rather, the point that I wish to emphasize is paying attention to what the student learns and how he learns it. This is significant so that the student does not build his knowledge and learning experience on incorrect premises and theories. What a student learns should be challenged and his understanding should be heightened rather than simply having the ability to regurgitate the information he was taught. This approach to learning is supported by the Prophetic traditions. It is narrated that the Holy Prophet (s) said, *"The endeavor of scholars is awareness [of what they learn] and the endeavor of fools is narration [without awareness]."*[10]

What is important is that we are conscious and aware of what we learn, not that we simply memorize without inquiry and scrutiny. This is where parents and guardians come into play in the elementary stages of a student's education, where the student is unable to differentiate because of their tender age. The guardian must guide the student through these stages and help foster the spirit of inquiry and awareness in him as he grows. That way, the more the student matures the greater their ability will be in distinguishing between information that is correct and incorrect – especially information that relies on history and narration.

## Our Perspective on Teachers

One of the most negative phenomena that exists in our society today is the apparent disrespect and disregard of teachers, which goes back to a number of reasons. In Islamic tradition, the teacher is regarded in one of the highest positions with the utmost respect. Dozens of our narrations emphasize the necessity of respecting, esteeming and being humble before his teacher. Islam has ordained a number of rights for teachers that must be observed, as outlined in the following narration from Imam Zein Al-Abideen (a):

---

[10] Al-Reyshahri, *Mizan Al-Hikma*, 3:2096.

*The rights of your teacher: respect your teacher and his session. Be eager to meet him and listen to him carefully. Speak to him politely and do not raise your voice above his. Do not answer questions that are asked of him until he answers. Do not converse during his gathering with anyone. Do not backbite any one before him. Defend your teacher if he is mentioned before you in an ill manner. Conceal his faults and express his virtues. Do not meet with his enemies and do not have enmity towards his friends. If you do this, the angels will testify that you sought him and learned his knowledge for the sake of God and not for the sake of people.*[11]

When we look back to our scholars we see the best examples in their regard and respect for their teachers. Our scholars would show respect to their teachers, regardless of their faith, so long as doing so would be a promotion of virtue as opposed to vice and of truth as opposed to falsehood.

It is said that one of our grand scholars was taught some lessons in mathematics by a Jewish teacher. Until the end of his life, whenever this scholar saw the Jewish teacher he would stand in respect and honor before him. He would say, "He is my teacher." This is the etiquette that Islam teaches us in regards to our teachers. We must raise our children to respect and honor their teachers instead of encouraging them to disobey them. To show dishonor and disrespect to our teachers and the teachers of our children is not becoming of us, especially as the followers of Ahlulbayt (a). Ahlulbayt (a) want us to be at the highest levels of eth-

---

[11] Al-Majlisi, *Bihar Al-Anwar*, 2:42.

ics, because ethics is a direct reflection of our creed and faith on the path of the Household of Muhammad (s).

# Islam's System of Worship

*In the Name of God, the Beneficent, the Merciful*

*Though they were not commanded except to worship God, dedicating their faith to Him as men of pure faith, and to maintain the prayer and pay the zakat. That is the upright religion.*[1]

We spoke in a previous chapter about the importance of worship in our daily lives and for mankind as a whole. In this chapter, we want to answer the following concerns:

If the ascension and excellence that can be attained through worship are wholly spiritual, why must we practice worships that involve more than our spirits? Why can't we simply reflect and supplicate in our hearts to reach that level? Why must we fast from dawn to dusk, or perform a pilgrimage to a specific place on Earth? Why must we make physical motions as part of our prayer?

---

[1] The Holy Quran. Chapter 16 [The Bees; Arabic: *Al-Nahl*]. Verse 43.

And why is the system of worship in Islam so static, that it has not seen any change since the time of the Prophet (s)? Why are we not given absolute freedom to innovate in the ways we wish to communicate with God? Why can't we change this system of worship to meet our needs?

## Worship is Meant for Body and Soul

The relationship between the body and the soul is a close one. Many bodily needs cannot be fulfilled without the spiritual aspect and many spiritual needs cannot be fulfilled without bodily actions. It is because of interconnection between the two that many acts of worship must be performed by the spirit using the body. There needs to be a balance between fulfilling the needs of the body and fulfilling the needs of the soul. We cannot neglect our spiritual wellbeing to fulfill only our bodily desires; that would certainly be a deviation from morality and possibly a sacrifice of eternal bliss. Neither can we neglect our body and focus only on spirituality, as that would lead to illness and weakness of the body. Our body is God's property and we do not have permission to abuse it as such. Hence, harming the body ultimately harms us spiritually as well.

Hunger, for example, is a bodily experience. However, it is also linked to spirituality. For example, we can reflect on our hunger to attain a greater realization of our true dependence on God. However, we cannot fulfill our hunger by simply imagining that we are full or by reflecting on the need for food. The body must be given its due right and allowed to consume food so that it can continue to operate properly.

This is a possible wisdom behind why we were given a system of worships that can achieve that required balance for us in our journey towards God. Effective worship is worship that advances the human being in light of the interconnectedness between the body and soul. Practicing acts of worship without a spiritual connection will not give us what we need. Nor will reflecting and meditating without the correct bodily acts of worship provide that balance that is required. It is narrated that the Commander of the Faithful (a) said, *"Instill in yourselves knowledge of the One who you worship, so that you can benefit with the movement of your limbs as you worship the One you know."*[2]

## The Constancy of the System of Worship

God, the All-Knowing, has encompassing knowledge of all creations before their creation and all events before their occurrence. *"No affliction visits the land or yourselves but it is in a Book before We bring it about – that is indeed easy for God."*[3]

God's knowledge encompasses all things in all places and across all times. He knows of everything before its creation, during its creation, and after its creation. Nothing escapes His knowledge. He knows of all changes and progress that mankind goes through. Still, God made the system of worships static. Despite all the changes that He knows will occur, He made the system constant, from the time of Prophet Muhammad (s) until the Day of Judgment. Yes, circumstances around these worships may change, and that does

---

[2] Al-Harrani, *Tuhaf Al-'Oqool*, 223.
[3] The Holy Quran. Chapter 57 [The Iron; Arabic: *Al-Hadeed*]. Verse 22.

not create any problem. God did not prohibit us from using manmade vehicles to reach our destination in the *Hajj*, for instance.

This constancy in the system of worship carries several pearls of wisdom:

*Preserving Social Cohesion*

Our system of worships plays an important role in preserving the very significant concept of social cohesion. It teaches us all to work together towards God and for His sake, sacrificing in the process our own personal gains for the common good. Islam places a great emphasis on communal worships, allowing the concept of communal interest to take root. Worships in Islam thus play a great role in reinforcing social cohesion and harmony, as well as a sense of sacrifice of personal benefits for the greater good. Unity in worship reinforces these concepts.

On the other hand, if we were to assume that we were given free rein to individually invent our personal modes of worship, these concepts would likely be lost. Each individual would worship as he likes and disregard all others. There would likely be no agreement on this issue, especially as it is so intimate to the individual. Society would likely lose a great factor that unites it, and gain instead a factor that may disunite it.

In one tradition, it is reported that Imam Sadiq (a) said:

> *Indeed, [God] has made communal prayers and [obligated] meeting for prayers so that [people] may know who prays and who does not pray, and who respects the times of prayers and who does not. Without this, no one would ever be*

*able to testify as to the virtue of anyone else. Whoever does not pray the communal prayers has no prayer among the Muslims. As the Messenger of God (s) said, 'there is no prayer for whoever does not pray with the Muslims in a mosque except for an exigency.*[4]

## Constancy Befits Worship

Because the goal of worship is to bring the individual closer to true servitude of God, worship must come in a form that befits and conforms to servitude. Servitude requires obedience to God's commands and abidance to His will. Giving individuals the choice of how to worship does not fall in line with this reality. Instilling the concept of servitude to God will take the individual higher in the levels of perfection. This comes through fulfillment of obligations and submission to the will of God. It is narrated that Imam Rida (a) described the purpose of worship as such, *"so that [people] do not become forgetful of His remembrance, nor depart from His etiquettes, nor disregard his commands and prohibitions…"*[5]

We are obligated to perform these worships whether we understand the specific reasoning behind them or not, and whether we know of the specific benefits or not. Yes, we do know the general reasoning behind worship and are aware of the general benefits of worship. God Almighty is the All-Wise. He would not command us without wisdom behind the command. But we do not need to know the specifics. This is why our scholars say that we must perform the obligations of worship "out of servitude" – meaning that we act simply because our Lord, God, has commanded us without

---

[4] Al-Sadouq, *'Ilal Al-Sharae'*, 2:325.
[5] Al-Sadouq, *'Oyun Akhbar al-Rida*, 2:110.

the need to know the specific benefits or particular wisdom behind the obligation. We cannot encompass God's infinite wisdom, and thus we cannot hope to understand all of the benefits that underlie every obligation. Rather, we simply perform these obligations out of obedience to God, declaring by that our servitude to Him.

There is no doubt that if we were to be given the choice of how and when to worship then for many of us that would have a negative effect on our level of servitude. We will begin to feel as if we can be independent of God, and as a result we will begin to distance ourselves from God. Furthermore, the fact is that worship increases our level of faith in the unseen, so that we can become closer to the level that Imam Ali (a) speaks about when he says, *"if the veil was to be removed, I would not increase in certainty."*[6] The first level of this certainty is belief in the unseen. We must hold fast to our belief in the unseen and obey the commands of God without doubting His wisdom.

## A Consistent Solution to Consistent Problems

Worship is a relationship between the worshipper and his lord. It's not a relationship between the individual and the environment. The relationship between and individual and his environment can change because of all the changes and technological advancements that have occurred. Instead of using an ox-drawn plow, we have many machines now to till the earth. Because mankind's abilities are changing and the environment is evolving, therefore the relationship between the two is constantly changing.

---

[6] Ibn Shahrashoub, *Al-Manaqib*, 1:317.

As for our relationship to God, it is a higher and spiritual connection that also has an impact on the relationships between individual humans. Therefore, the system of worship that is dictated by the relationship of man to God solves constant issues and fulfills the perpetual demands of mankind. When needs are constant the means to satisfy those needs must also be constant. And when we look at worships, we see that they have general and specific effects. The general effect is that worship fulfills certain needs for mankind; each specific act of worship has its own effect which results in the fulfillment of certain individual needs or its provides solutions for problems afflicting humanity.

As for the general effects of worship, we see that humanity has a desire and a need to belong and connect with a higher being; with perfection. Some of our scholars explain this issue as such:

> [An individual is in need of worship] to continue his path of ascension and so that he does not lose his way – due to not feeling any belonging [to a higher being] – or becomes complacent and staggers, or even falls in the pits of polytheism and fanaticism. This would be the effect of changing the limited relative connections he has in this world to absolutes, so that he stops at them in his journey. Worship is a practical expression of belonging to the absolute. It fosters in the individual his faith in God through practice of worships that re-emphasize this belonging. At the same time, this worship rejects all other [concepts as non-absolute] and all other false deities.[7]

---

[7] Al-Hakim, *Daur Ahlulbayt fi Bina al-Jama'a al-Saliha*, 2:160.

Another of our great scholars also says:

> *Worship is the one that deepens this feeling [towards the higher being] as it is a practical expression that combines both affirmation [of God's existence] and rejection [of all other false deities]... When someone starts his prayer with 'God is Great,' he accentuates this rejection. When he declares in his prayers that his Prophet (s) is '[God's] servant and messenger,' he accentuates this rejection. When he fasts and refrains from the necessities of life for the sake of God and as a challenge to his desires, he accentuates this rejection.*[8]

Belonging to the absolute is a constant need, yet we cannot belong to the true absolute without practically expressing this belonging. This expression must be constant to strengthen and deepen this relationship. God has chosen the forms of worship so that they are the best means to reach this end. If there were better means to do this, God would have provided us with them.

As for the specific effects of worships, we see that each type of worship has a certain benefit and plays a role in achieving the lofty goals of the human self. This is seen in the Quran and the narrations of the Holy Household (a). For example, we see that the Quran tells us that prayers are a means to averting deviation – God says *"Indeed the prayer restrains from indecent and wrongful conduct."*[9] As for fasting, God says, *"O you*

---

[8] Al-Sadr, *Al-Fatawa Al-Wadhiha*, 713.
[9] The Holy Quran. Chapter 29 [The Spider; Arabic: *Al-'Ankabout*]. Verse 45.

*who have faith! Prescribed for you is fasting as it was prescribed for those who were before you, so that you may be God-wary.*"[10]

We find in the sermon of Lady Zahra (a) a reference to different types of worships, along with all the specific effects that each one has. She says, "... *God has obligated faith as a purification from polytheism, prayers as a cleansing from pride, alms as an increase in blessings, fasting as an expression of dedication, the pilgrimage as an elevation of faith, and justice as harmony for the hearts....*"[11]

And there are numerous narrations as such and anyone interested can refer back to the book "Ilal Al-Sharae'" for Sheikh Al-Sadouq.

So every act of worship has its own effects and benefits and deals with a distinct aspect of human life. That is why it is said that worships in Islam are encompassing of all aspects of human life. Indeed, as our scholars have said,

> *[Worships in Islam are] encompassing of all aspects of human life; individual, social, economic, and political. Furthermore, Islam has called for all of man's activities to be done in devotion [to God], even in food, drink, pleasures, and desires that each individual loves. The door for seeking proximity to God is open. Man can emphasize his relationship with God in all his actions and activities [through devotion to God in intention].*[12]

---

[10] The Holy Quran. Chapter 2 [The Cow; Arabic: *Al-Baqara*]. Verse 183.
[11] Al-Amili. *Wasael Al-Shia*, 1:22. See also: Al-Sadouq, *Man La Yahdaruh Al-Faqih*, 3:568.
[12] Al-Hakim, *Daur Ahlulbayt fi Bina al-Jama'a al-Saliha*, 2:162.

# Prayer

*In the Name of God the Beneficent the Merciful*

*Be watchful of your prayers, and [especially] the middle prayer, and stand in obedience to God.*[1]

Worship plays an important role in a person's life and happiness. God neither needs people's worship nor does He benefit from it. God Almighty is the Ultimate Cause, upon whom every other being depends. The worship of a servant does not benefit God nor does the sin of a disobeyer harm Him. "*O mankind! You are the ones who stand in need of God, and God—He is the All-sufficient, the All-laudable.*"[2] However, because of God's compassion towards his servants, He sends the Messengers to show the path to seek closeness to Him. He made the system of worship one of the most important means and tools to attain his satisfaction and nearness. One of the most important worships is Prayer, which is the key pillar that Islam was built on. It is reported by credible sources that the Prophet (s) stated just before his death, "*One who takes his prayers lightly is not from me and will not reach*

---

[1] The Holy Quran. Chapter 2 [The Cow; Arabic: *Al-Baqara*]. Verse 238.
[2] The Holy Quran. Chapter 35 [Arabic: *Fatir*]. Verse 15.

*the heavenly spring, I swear by God...*"³ Being attentive to one's prayers is actually the final will of the various Prophets (s) sent by God.⁴

Prayer is so highly prescribed that God Almighty has made it obligatory from the day a person becomes religiously accountable until the day a person departs this world. Even during a person's last moments in this life, he must perform it. Yes, the form and manner in which prayer is offered in situations of necessity and physical disability may vary, but the obligation remains nonetheless. The books of jurisprudence present to us the specific rulings that apply to the one that is drowning or burning and how they should perform their prayer, for instance. Furthermore, even in extreme situations such as battle, prayer remains an obligation. Thus, if Prayer is obligatory in such circumstances, then performing it under normal circumstances is even more pressing.

The discussion about Prayer is expansive due to the many aspects that can be discussed. We attempt here to shed light on only some of the aspects that are related to Prayer. The Commander of the Faithful (a) shows the significance of this great worship and the role it plays in a person's life where he states,

> *Commit to Prayer; maintain it; increase in performing it and seek closeness [to God] through it. For it is indeed a timed prescription for the faithful. Do you not hear the answers of the people of hellfire when they were questioned,* 'What has brought you into hell?' They shall say: 'We were not of those who prayed.' *Prayer peels off*

---

³ Al-Sadouq, *'Ilal al-Sharae'*, 2:356.
⁴ Al-Kulayni, *Al-Kafi*, 3:264

*sins like leaves are peeled off [trees] and it releases [the hold of] sins like the release of a tight rope. The Prophet (s) described it as a hot spring at one's door: A person bathes himself from it during the day and night five times - what possible dirt could be left on him... There are men among the believers who understood its right. These are men who are not distracted by the ornaments of worldly provisions or the comfort of children or money. God the Al-Mighty states,* 'by men whom neither trading nor bargaining distracts from the remembrance of God, and the maintenance of prayer and the giving of zakat.'[5]

What drives us to speak about these aspects of prayer is to motivate the believers to take care of their prayers because many people are negligent and careless about this great obligation and undermine its value. Many people prioritize other tasks and obligations before Prayer. Moreover, for some people, prayer only comes after even the trifles of this life, which have no comparable value for a person, such as a video game, movie, and television show. A believer is supposed to be concerned about his commitment to this great obligation due to the significant impact it has on his present and future in this life and the hereafter. This will be clarified when we discuss the reasons why Prayer is significant.

## Why is Prayer so Important?

When we discuss the issue of the significance of Prayer, we must mention that we are not claiming that these reasons are necessarily the actual and real causes driving the Divine

---

[5] Al-Radi, *Nahj Al-Balagha*, 2:179.

legislation of prayer. Whatever comes to us from the Divine Legislator we ought to accept without the need to know the specific reason as to why it is important. True worship of God makes the servant accept what the Master requests without need for understanding the particular reasons or specific causes. That is because the servant, no matter how much intellectual strength he has, might not comprehend many of the affairs and metaphysical effects of worship and its role in his future, the hereafter. However, through referencing the Holy Scripture relating to Prayer, we can understand some pieces of wisdom signifying the importance of prayer. While these points of wisdom are not an exhaustive explanation for the legislation of prayer, they do address to some extent the role of prayer and it impact on major changes in a believer's life. Therefore, these things might be part of the reasons that dictate the significance of Prayer. Amongst them are the following.

*Preventing Indecency and Vice*

This issue is addressed in the Holy Quran where God states, *"Recite what has been revealed to you of the Book, and maintain the prayer. Indeed the prayer restrains from indecent and wrongful conduct, and the remembrance of God is surely greater. And God knows whatever [deeds] you do."*[6]

A person is instructed in this life to do what is consistent with God's teachings so that he can live a proper life and attain eternal happiness in the hereafter. Perhaps, the greatest thing that causes a person to drift away from God is indecency and vice. Anything that is of indecency and vice,

---

[6] The Holy Quran. Chapter 29 [The Spider; Arabic: *Al-Ankaboot*]. Verse 45.

from major to minor sins, results in a person being far from God. Here, the role of Prayer comes in to make the servant stand before his Lord remembering Him. No doubt this will play a vital role in reminding one of God and also reminding him of the strict surveillance surrounding him by God where He does not miss even an atom's worth of a deed. Consequently, this daily meeting and constant remembrance makes a person distant from all that angers God, if one truly understands the meaning of Prayer. A person that prays will eventually benefit from his prayer distancing him from indecency and vice. It is narrated that a young companion of the Prophet (s) used to pray with the Prophet (s) and commit indecencies. This was conveyed to the Prophet (s) to which he replied, *"His Prayer will prevent him one day." It was not long before he repented."*[7]

We can take an analogy from our materialistic life in order to further clarify the idea. If a person knows that he will meet an important figure that plays a key role and has an impact on his life, and that this person will be able to access his personal files and will become aware of some of his affairs that will displease him, we will find that this person will be very protective to ensure that what reaches this important figure is only that which will please him. For no matter how much one is under surveillance, the surveillance will only capture some of his conduct. However, pertaining to what goes on with him internally, it is impossible to discover it. Nonetheless, one lives with anxiety and fear trying to please those who impact his life. Similarly, how can a person live in such a state where he faces God five times a

---

[7] Al-Majlisi, *Bihar Al-Anwar*, 79:198.

day and meets with him five times. Where God is aware of all of His creations' actions, small and big, He knows of any individual's thoughts and feelings. In addition, God knows that the person is in need of Him in every moment and aspect of his life. If a person is able to think this way, he will realize the impact of his prayer in becoming closer to God.

## *Purification from Arrogance*

Many individuals tend to be materialistic and lead materialistic lives, which they affect and are affected by. The effects of such surrounding are at times so great that such individuals lose sight of their weaknesses and deficiencies. This person may become headless of his reality where he perceives that he is able to accomplish things himself, independent of God Almighty. When he increases in wealth, he thinks that he is the one that managed to earn the money with his intelligence and ability, and forgets that the favor in this goes back to God and that without the favor of God, he would not have been able to gain anything. For true power and strength is in the hands of God. Similarly, a so-called scholar might think along the same lines where the knowledge that he receives is through his own intellectual ability. Many such individuals that make achievements, whether monetary or intellectual, show arrogance and conceit to others who have not attained what they have. Heedlessness and arrogance are grave diseases that a person can be inflicted with because they are barriers that prevent one from properly observing reality. Additionally, arrogance is a major reason that causes a person to lose the hereafter because it is one of the major sins and it invokes God's wrath. Moreover, it leads one at times to commit blasphemy and it is one of the primary causes for a host of problems between people. So many wars and disasters that humanity suffered from we find were caused by arrogance and conceit. For a person who is granted some strength begins to believe that he must subjugate others as he sees himself superior to the rest. Thus, the arrogance can change from a personal affliction to a societal plague. Moreover, it can expand to become a universal disease that all of humanity suffers from.

Here comes the role of Prayer to return the person to his true self, to reality, and the remembrance of God and the necessity of submitting unconditionally to Him. When he stands before God, he stands as a servant before his Master and shows the perfect submission and devotion and observes in himself the true need of God. This is specifically the case in congregational Prayer, which has a major impact in eradicating this disease. In congregational prayer, you have the great and the inferior, the wealthy and poor, the scholar and ignorant, the old and young, all stand in one line before the Great Creator displaying true obedience and absolute loyalty to Him. Furthermore, the Prayer consists of exercises in submission and worship, such as adoration and prostration, and acts glorifying the Great and consecrating Him. This is a process that is repeated at least five times a day, and is subject to increase with recommended prayers, all of which calls upon a person to reflect and contemplate regarding his reality. This reality is that he is a servant that does not control his fate and that he does not have any power and strength except in God, The Supreme, and The Great. The master of the believers Ali (a) refers to this reality by stating, "The obligation of faith purifies from polytheism and Prayer cleanses from arrogance."[8]

## Atoning Sins

It is narrated on behalf of the Prophet (s),

> *I heard a caller [calling out] upon the presence of each Prayer: Oh sons of Adam stand and extinguish [the fires] that you have lit upon yourselves. They then stand and [ritually] purify [themselves], upon which their sins fall from their eyes. They pray and [their sins] between the two are forgiven. Then, you light [fire] in between that. When it is the time of the first Prayer, the caller calls: oh sons of Adam, stand and extinguish [the fires] that you have lit upon yourself. So they stand, [ritually] purify [themselves], and pray. Upon which, [their sins] in between the two are forgiven. When the afternoon Prayer arrives, the same occurs, when the sunset Prayer arrives, the same occurs, and when the evening Prayer arrives, the same occurs. They then sleep and their sins have been forgiven.*[9]

It may be difficult for a typical believer to avoid sin completely because he does not have an iron will and has thus not qualified for the special knowledge of an Immaculate one. So long as he lives within society, he is exposed to various testing factors. He might not be intending to fall into these forbidden acts, but at one point or another he may find himself in a position of weakness and God forbid slip into sin. If God wanted to judge us based on a balance of justice, then our sins would surely tip the balance and we

---

[8] Al-Radi, *Nahj Al-Balagha*, 4:55.
[9] Al-Majlisi, *Bihar Al-Anwar*, 79:224.

would deserve to be punished. That is even with the divine formula taken into account. What is meant by the divine formula here is that God multiplies a good deed by 10 and counts a bad deed as only one. Even with that formula in place, many have enough sins to tip the balance against their favor. If we return to our true reality and judge ourselves as a rival would, we would find that we have shortcomings and are sinners no matter how hard we attempt to find justifications for ourselves. *"Indeed, man is a witness to himself, though he should offer excuses [to justify his failings]."*[10]

Here comes the compassion of God, who encompasses the disobedient servant with His forgiveness and pleasure and provides him with avenues to rid himself of these sins and the fire that surrounds him. This is articulated by the Prophet (s), *"Stand and extinguish [the fires] that you have lit upon yourselves."* When a person commits sin, he lights the fire upon himself and the way to put out this fire is through Prayer; and the generosity and mercy of God, which encompasses everything, grants a person what extinguish this fire, which he lit upon himself. From here, arises this great concern in performing Prayer on time because it is the immediate extinguishment of fire. The longer the fire is going, the greater the damage. Thus, one must hurry to extinguish it. However, we must pay attention to three matters.

First, some of the narrations announce that the role of Prayer is to remove the effect of minor sins, and not every sin – as a narration attributed to Imam Ali (a) indicates – *"The five Prayers are an atonement for what is done in between them,*

---

[10] The Holy Quran. Chapter 75 [Arabic: *Al-Qiyama*]. Verse 14, 15.

*so long as one avoids major sins. And this is what God says: 'Indeed good deeds efface misdeeds. That is an admonition for the mindful.'"*[11]

Second, these narrations do not mean that a person can blatantly commit sins as long as he performs his Prayer, thinking that the prayer will atone them. Indeed, insisting on committing minor sins in itself is a major sin. Furthermore, insisting on committing any sin intentionally is to challenge God's authority and belittle it. The size of the sin becomes irrelevant when one measures it against the Grandeur of the One we are sinning against. It has been reported that the Prophet (s) said, *"Do not look at [how small] the sin is, but rather look at who it is that you sinned against."*[12]

Third, we must also pay attention to the fact that only those prayers which are accepted by god are capable of expunging sins. If the Prayer is not accepted then there is no guarantee that the Prayer will take care of our sins. The Prayer that we offer may be legally valid, in terms of the rules and conditions pertaining to Prayer. That relieves us of our religious legal obligation, but does not necessarily the Prayer is accepted by God Almighty. It is narrated that the Prophet (s) said, *"There are some prayers in which half of the prayer is accepted, [others] one-third, [others] one-fourth, [others] one-fifth… and [others] one-tenth [is accepted]. And some prayers are folded like a worn-out [piece of] clothing and the face of [the one who performed that prayer] is struck with it. The only [part] you gain from your Prayer is that which you turn toward wholeheartedly."*[13]

---

[11] Al-Nouri, *Mustadrak al-Wasael*, 3:15.

[12] Al-Tusi, *Al-Amali*, 528.

[13] Al-Nouri, *Mustadrak Al-Wasael*, 3:59.

## BARRIERS TO ACCEPTED PRAYERS

It is noteworthy to discuss some of the reasons why some Prayers may not be accepted, as is stated in the narrations of the Prophet (s) and his Holy Household (a).

*Dishonoring the Parents*

One of the most significant reasons why Prayer is not accepted is dishonoring one's parents, which is to cause them pain and displeasure. God Almighty commanded that one must be good towards one's parents just as He commanded that one obey Him, worship Him, and not associate partners with Him. God Almighty states,

> *Say, 'Come, I will recount what your Lord has forbidden you. That you shall not ascribe any partners to Him, and you shall be good to the parents, you shall not kill your children due to penury—We will provide for you and for them—you shall not approach indecencies, the outward among them and the inward ones, and you shall not kill a soul [whose life] God has made inviolable, except with due cause. This is what He has enjoined upon you so that you may exercise your reason.*[14]

God will not accept the Prayers of someone who displeases his parents and hurts them when they want the best for him. Imam Al-Sadiq's narration in this context is striking where he states, "*Whoever looks at his parents with disgust – [even if] while they have oppressed him – God will not accept his Prayers.*"[15]

---

[14] The Holy Quran. Chapter 6 [The Cattle; Arabic: *Al-An'aam*]. Verse 151.
[15] Al-Kulayni, *Al-Kafi*, 2:349.

Here, we must point to the danger of this issue, especially in our contemporary world, where we find many children belittling their parents. Some falsely think that their education and social status justifies their disrespect to their parents. Money has blinded many in society, causing them to forget the importance of their parents. Thus, they proceed to look upon them with disrespect and neglect. Perhaps social tendencies have imposed a specific reality that distances people from honoring their parents. It may be so much so that – as is mentioned in newspapers and magazines – there are cases where parents are left alone in elderly homes without any care or attention. What good is in such a child?! One must realize that any blessings he enjoys is due to the favor of his parents, after God. One's parents are the cause of an individual's upbringing in this life. There are a wide range of verses and narrations that speak about the status of parents and importance of taking care of them. From here, it is logical to conclude that God does not accept the Prayers of a person that does not fulfill his obligation towards his parents and neglects their service.

*Backbiting*

This widely spread disease in the community is dangerous and extreme in inflicting most people. One who studies society finds – unfortunately – that this phenomenon is visible even among believers. Many practice it without realizing its dangers and the great sin that one commits by engaging in this ill behavior. The Holy Quran describes backbiting as eating a dead brother's flesh,

> *O you who have faith! Avoid much suspicion; indeed some suspicions are sins. And do not spy on one another or*

*backbite. Will any of you love to eat the flesh of his dead brother? You would hate it. Be wary of God; indeed God is all-clement, all-merciful.*[16]

From this point, we must pay attention to these types of sins, which prevent the acceptance of Prayer. It is narrated by the Prophet (s), *"Whoever backbites a Muslim, God will not accept his Prayers and fast for forty days and nights except if the person forgives him."*[17]

## Neglecting Prayers

Neglecting Prayer, meaning not giving it importance and not feeling its significance, can prevent our Prayers from being accepted. We find that some deal with their Prayers based on their changing mood. Whenever he desires, he performs his Prayer and whenever his mood does not support that, he stops. In practice, he does not deal with it as a religious obligation that he must fulfill. No doubt, undermining Prayers means in one way or another undermining its legislator. If a person fears God, he will not be negligent in performing his Prayer – an act that the Divine Legislator emphasized on the importance and necessity of being committed to. Not maintaining and committing to Prayer means that it is not important to the person. That is why we find that the Divine Legislator equates undermining and not maintaining prayer equivalent to abandoning it. Thus, this Prayer is not accepted, as it is reported that Imam al-Sadiq (s) stated,

---

[16] The Holy Quran. Chapter 49 [Arabic: *Al-Hujurat*]. Verse 12.
[17] Al-Majlisi, *Bihar Al-Anwar*, 72:258.

> *By God, a person may live for 50 years without having [even] a single Prayer accepted by God. What is harsher than this?! By God, you know that there are those among your neighbors and friends who if they were to pray to some of you, [you] would not accept it from that person had they taken it lightly. God does not accept but that which is good. How can He accept that which is taken lightly?*[18]

We must point that the barriers for the acceptance of Prayer are not limited to what we have discussed. Rather, there are other factors that also prevent the acceptance of Prayer, as is mentioned by some of the Great Jurists,

> *One must avoid the things that prevent the acceptance of Prayer such as self-admiration, [feeling like one is doing God a favor], not paying obligatory alms, violating [marital rights], running away [from one's obligation toward those who have rights over him/her], envy [wishing ill to others], arrogance, backbiting, consuming that which is forbidden, drinking intoxicants, and, rather, all sins because God says, 'God accepts only from the God wary.*[19] [20]

---

[18] Al-Kulayni, *Al-Kafi*, 3:269.
[19] The Holy Quran. Chapter 5 [The Spread; Arabic: *Al-Maeda*]. Verse 27.
[20] Al-Yazdi, *Al-Urwat Al-Wuthqa*, 3:28.

# REVERENCE

*In the Name of God the Beneficent the Merciful*

*Certainly, the faithful have attained salvation—those who are [reverent] in their prayers, avoid vain talk, carry out their [duty of] zakat, guard their private parts, (except from their spouses or their slave women, for then they are not blameworthy; but whoever seeks [anything] beyond that—it is they who are transgressors), and those who keep their trusts and covenants and are watchful of their prayers. It is they who will be the inheritors, who shall inherit paradise and will remain in it [forever].*[1]

No believer should doubt that prayer is absolutely one of the greatest and most important acts. Religious texts emphasize this and highlight the position of prayer over other worships. We previously spoke about prayer and its importance; here, we will delve into the particulars of prayers that bear special qualifications. Namely, we want to study prayers offered "with the presence of the heart"; the prayer of those with reverence for God. God refers to those who

---

[1] The Holy Quran. Chapter 23 [The Believers; Arabic: *Al-Mu'minoon*]. Verses 1-11.

offer such prayers as "maintaining the prayers." That is why we see that in many of the ziyarat (salutations) directed towards the Holy Household (a) reference to this phrase, "I bear witness that you have maintained the prayers...." This term – maintaining the prayers – has a meaning different from what we usually imagine. We understand maintaining the prayers as performing the daily prayers with all their parts and rituals. Each of us thinks that he is maintaining his prayers. But if it was so, there would be no exclusivity for the Imams (a) and their righteous followers in the term, as implied by the salutations addressing them.

Maintaining the prayers means that they are performed in their most perfect and sublime form, exactly as God intended. That is, it must be performed with complete reverence for God.

One of the first descriptions of the believers who have attained the pleasure of God and who will inherit the everlasting gardens of Paradise is that they are reverent in their prayers. It is interesting to note that the characteristics of the believers that were outlined in the verses above began and ended at the same point. They began with the characteristic of reverence in prayer, and ended in being watchful of prayer. This is perhaps an indication of the great role of prayer and its importance in achieving God's pleasure.

What is required of a believer is not just to perform prayers completely with all the attributes that make it legally valid. Rather, a believer should perform prayer in a fashion that would earn him the rank of "maintainer of prayer." This comes through reverence in prayer. Still, many of us lack this quality. We do not distinguish the difference between a merely valid prayer and a prayer that is not only valid but also accepted by God. The valid or correct prayer is the complete prayer that consists of all the parts, and is enough to relieve the individual of the religious responsibility to pray. However, an accepted prayer is the one that has an effect on the person and keeps him from sin and deviance. That is the type of prayer that God refers to when He says, *"Recite what has been revealed to you of the Book, and maintain the prayer. Indeed the prayer restrains from indecent and wrongful conduct, and the remembrance of God is surely greater. And God knows whatever [deeds] you do."*[2]

This is the prayer that fulfills the requirements of reverence for and hope in God. This is why we see the narrations stating that each man will receive from his prayer to the extent that he puts reverence for and hope in God into it. One of the companions of Imam Sajjad (a) narrates the following,

> *I saw Ali the son of Hussein (a) praying. In his prayer, his robe fell over his shoulder, but he did not adjust it until he completed his prayers. When I asked him about this he said,* 'Woe to you! In the presence of whom was I? Indeed, the only [part] that is accepted from a servant's Prayer is that [part] of it which one turns toward wholeheartedly.'[3]

What is required of a person is not to simply perform the acts and rituals of worship. Rather, it is the quality and sincerity of these acts that matter most. It is narrated that the Commander of the Faithful (a) said, *"The importance is not in that you pray, fast, and pay alms. Rather, the importance is in per-*

---

[2] The Holy Quran. Chapter 29 [The Spider; Arabic: *Al-'Ankaboot*]. Verse 45.
[3] Al-Majlisi, *Bihar Al-Anwar*, 81:237.

*forming prayers with a pious heart, actions that are pleasing to God, and an upright reverence."*[4]

## WHAT IS REVERENCE?

We use the word "reverence" in this book as a translation of the Arabic word *"Khushu'."* The English word reverence means "honor or respect felt or shown… profound adoring awed respect"[5] Every servant must have reverence for the Lord arising out of a deep awareness of God's presence. This awareness instills a level of fear of God, not because God is out to get us but because God Almighty's presence is so overpowering. One with proper awareness would not want to fall out of God's favor. The more an individual comes to know of God and His majesty, His great power, and the greatness of His names and attributes, the more he grows fearful of Him, in a sense. That is why God says, *"Only those of God's servants having knowledge fear Him."*[6]

It is narrated that the Prophet (s) was asked about reverence, to which he replied, *"Humility in prayers and that a servant approaches wholeheartedly towards God."*[7]

Approaching God wholeheartedly means that we empty our hearts of anything but Him. This is not an easy task. It requires great spiritual training and discipline. It is not an impossible level to achieve, but neither is it an easy one. It requires determination, will, perseverance, and constant spir-

---

[4] Ibid, 81:230.
[5] Marriam Webster Dictionary.
[6] The Holy Quran. Chapter 35 [Arabic: *Fatir*]. Verse 28.
[7] Al-Majlisi, *Bihar Al-Anwar*, 81:264.

itual training so that this high level of dedication can be achieved.

In explaining the verse, *"those who are [reverent] in their prayers,"*[8] our scholars have said:

> *They are submissive [to God], humble, and servile. They do not raise their gaze from their place of prostration. They do not turn right and left. It is narrated that the Prophet (s) saw a man playing with his beard in prayer, so he said, 'Surely, if his heart was reverent his limbs would have been reverent as well." This contains an indication that reverence in prayer is a matter of both the heart and the limbs. As for the heart, it is effectuated through full dedication of the heart towards [the prayer], and avoiding all else; so that it is empty of everything but the worship and the [One who is] worshipped. As for the limbs, [reverence] is effectuated through lowering the gaze, not turning around and not twiddling.*[9]

Some scholars have also said,

> *Reverence, according to the verses of the Quran is: [1] the reverence of sight as in the verse* 'they will emerge from the graves as if they were scattered locusts with a [reverent] look [in their eyes]'[10]; *[2] the reverence of the heart as in the verse* 'Is it not time yet for those who have faith that their hearts should be [reverent] for God's remembrance and toward the truth which has come down [to them], and to be not like

---

[8] The Holy Quran. Chapter 23 [The Believers; Arabic: *Al-Mu'minoon*]. Verse 2.
[9] Al-Reyshahri, *Mizan Al-Hikma*, 2:1633. Citing: Al-Tabrasi, *Majma' Al-Bayan*, 7:176.
[10] The Holy Quran. Chapter 54 [The Moon; Arabic: *Al-Qamar*]. Verse 7.

those who were given the Book before? Time took its toll on them and so their hearts were hardened, and many of them are transgressors"*11*; and *[3] the reverence of speech as in the verse* "On that day they will follow a summoner in whom there will be no deviousness. The voices will be muted before the All-beneficent, and you will hear nothing but a murmur."*12* *Reverence in prayer bears all three of these meanings.*13

This is the reverence that the Quran describes. It is reverence of the heart, sight, and voice that forms a holistic reverence towards God. These are the manifestations of sensing God's greatness. These gestures are the appropriate reactions to the realization that one is standing in the presence of the Lord of the heavens and the earth who knows all that passes in his heart and is closer to him then his very own self.

## How can I Achieve Reverence?

The most important factor for achieving reverence is having presence of the heart and vacating it of all things aside from sincerity in seeking God's pleasure. You must feel that you are standing in His presence. You must speak with him by the words of the Quran and the supplications. This is not an easy task; reaching this state requires great efforts.

---

[11] The Holy Quran. Chapter 57 [The Iron; Arabic: *Al-Hadeed*]. Verse 16.
[12] The Holy Quran. Chapter 20 [Arabic: *Ta Ha*]. Verse 108.
[13] Al-Reyshahri, *Mizan Al-Hikma*, 2:1633.

So why should we strive to achieve this state if we can get by with simple performance of the required acts? Simply doing the required acts that make prayer legally valid may save us from punishment. But there is so much more beyond that! The levels of Paradise and the stations of closeness to God Almighty require more than a merely legally valid prayer. Being saved from drowning is one thing, but enjoying the various blessings of land, sea, air, and beyond is something else. Striving to achieve the state of reverence is doable with God's support. The truth of the matter is that God urges us to expend our efforts in attempting to reach that state. God says, *"As for those who strive in Us, We shall surely guide them in Our ways,"*[14] *"As for him who gives and is Godwary and confirms the best promise, We shall surely ease him into facility."*[15] Simply performing the acts of prayer without the due reverence to God may not be sufficient to reap the intended fruits of prayer, especially if it is thrown back at its doer; it is narrated that Imam Baqir (a) said, *"you do not gain anything of your prayer except [the part] of it which you turn toward [wholeheartedly]. If a person is distracted throughout it all or neglects to perform [its actions or etiquettes], it is folded and [that person] is hit on the face with it."*[16]

There are a number of things that help us reach this state of reverence. Observing these matters sprouts from some recognition of the value in prayer within us, and also in turn contributes to fostering the state of reverence within us. They include:

---

[14] The Holy Quran. Chapter 29 [The Spider; Arabic: *Al-'Ankaboot*]. Verse 69.
[15] The Holy Quran. Chapter 92 [The Night; Arabic: *Al-Layl*]. Verses 5-7.
[16] Al-Majlisi, *Bihar Al-Anwar*, 81:260.

## Observing the Time of Prayer

Observing the time of prayer is one of the important issues that the holy texts have emphasized. It shows the importance that a person gives to this great worship. There is no doubt that giving attention to any matter is an indication of a person's attachment to that thing. It reflects a sense of responsibility to perform it in the way God wishes for us to perform it. The traditions in this regard are countless. It is reported that Imam Ali (a) said,

> *There is no act more beloved to God than prayers. Do not be distracted from their set times by any of the matters of the world. God the exalted chastised nations by saying* "but [they] are heedless of their prayers," *meaning that they were neglectful and took lightly their set times.*[17]

It is also narrated that he (a) said, *"preserve the five prayers in their set times, as they are to God the Exalted in a [high] position."*[18]

Observing these set times of prayers will mean that the individual gradually begins to set aside this time for worship. He will begin to change his schedule and tasks so that they are agreeable to that set time for worship.

One who does not care to perform the prayer at its due time does not care much for the prayer prescribed by God as a whole. It does not represent to such a person a matter of great importance. Such an individual is in danger of becoming neglectful of prayers, and neglecting one's prayers is a grave sin. It is narrated that Imam Baqir (a) said, "do not be neglectful of your prayers. The Prophet (s) said at his

---

[17] Ibid, 10:100.
[18] Al-Majlisi, *Bihar Al-Anwar*, 74:293.

deathbed, '*Whoever takes his prayers lightly is not from [my followers]....*"[19]

The vast majority of us will prioritize many things over prayers. This is where we must ask: 'how can a person be reverent of God when he does not give prayers the most basic priority and attention that comes by performing it at its set time?

*Observing the Etiquettes and Prerequisites of Prayer*

In order to foster a sense of reverence toward God in prayer, one should attempt to perform it with all of its etiquettes and prerequisites. If a person wishes to achieve excellence in any action of his daily life, he will do anything that will improve the quality of that action. For a person to nurture a sense of reverence in prayer, he should observe its prerequisites; Wudhu, Adhan, Iqama, and all the other recommended actions that come before the prayer. These actions leading up to prayer can instill a sense of the importance of the prayer in the heart of the person.

A person should prepare himself mentally before approaching the prayer. He must begin to sense that he is standing in the hands of God. This comes through taking the practical steps that create a high spiritual sense and environment. This may be what the narration of Imam Ali (a) alludes to when it relates, "*there is no prayer without performing Wudhu properly [giving each part of it its due right], mindful awareness of the intention, sheer certainty, emptying the heart [of anyone but God], and*

---

[19] Al-Kulayni, *Al-Kafi*, 3:269.

*foregoing [all other] matters."*²⁰ Indeed, God says *"So when you are done, exert yourself, and turn eagerly to your Lord."*²¹

Performing Wudhu properly, giving each part of it its due right plays a role in prayer's completeness, as no act can be complete and perfect without a complete and perfect prerequisite. When we also look at the narrations in regards to Adhan and Iqama and their role in the completeness of prayer and its rewards, we see that they can also play an important role in giving the individual a sense of prayer's importance. This in turn can create a feeling of reverence towards God during prayer. It is narrated that the Prophet (s) in his will to Abuthar said,

> *Oh Abuthar, your Lord would boast of three types of individuals before His angels. [First] a person who, in a desolate land, performs Adhan and Iqama and then prays. Your Lord would say to the angels 'look at My servant, praying while no one sees him but Me.' Then seventy thousand angels would descend to pray behind him, and they would ask forgiveness for him until the next day.... Oh Abuthar, if a person is in a desolate land and performs his Wudhu or Tayammum, then performs Adhan and Iqama, and prays, God would command the angels to line up behind him in a row where neither of its ends is visible [due to its length]. They would bow upon his bowing, prostrate upon his prostration, and [ask God to answer] his supplications. Oh Abuthar, whoever performs Iqama but not Ad-*

---

²⁰ Al-Majlisi, *Bihar Al-Anwar*, 81:243.
²¹ The Holy Quran. Chapter 94 [Arabic: *Al-Sharh*]. Verses 7 and 8.

*han*, no angels will pray with him but his two angels that accompany him.²²

This is in addition to the great blessings and rewards that the prerequisites hold in and of themselves. An individual's observance of these prerequisites indicates the extent of the importance of prayers to him. How great is the difference between the individual that performs the prayer with all of its etiquettes and prerequisites and a person that performs his prayer without them? There is no doubt that observance of these etiquettes sprouts from and contributes to a distinct flavor and joy in prayer that is not tasted by a person who is performing the prayers in haste as if he seeks only to relieve himself of a burden.

*Specifying a Place of Worship*

In order to feel the importance of prayer, a person should designate a special place for his prayers. This is a matter encouraged by the narrations. The secret in this may lie in the fact that specifying a space for prayers gives a person a sense of special significance when standing in it. It may also be so that this specified space is empty of all other distractions so that a person's mind would not be preoccupied by things around him, or some other wisdom. It is narrated that Imam Sadiq (a) wrote to one of his companions,

> *I would love for you to make in your house a mosque in one of [its rooms]. [Before you pray, put on] clothes that are worn and coarse. Then ask God to free you from the hellfire*

---

²² Al-Amili, *Wasael Al-Shia*, 5:383.

*and to have you to enter paradise. And do not speak any wrong or any word of corruption.*[23]

When a person enters the special place in his home that he has set aside for worship, he may begin to feel that he is in a state different from all others; this is not a time of distraction with food or sleep, but a time for worship.

Our Holy Imams (a) used to take the place that would be more befitting of a sense of weakness and servility in their worship of God. For example, on a dark night, the tyrant *Mutawakkil*'s guards stormed the residence of Imam al-Hadi (s) in search of weapons and letters from supporters. They initially found nothing of the sort... But then the guards opened the door of a closed off room, only to find the holy Imam; their gazes rested upon the Imam (s) – who was dressed in wool, sitting on the sand and gravel, and directing himself toward the Almighty while reciting verses from the Holy Scripture.[24]

These factors, when practiced wisely, can draw the individual closer to a state of reverence for God in prayers. These factors should be practiced with care and should not themselves become a reason to be distracted from God Almighty.

## *Pray as if it is Your Last*

Another factor that allows us to sense the importance of prayers is putting ourselves in the following scenario: Imagine that this prayer that you are performing is the last prayer that you will perform before you depart this world – may

---

[23] Al-Majlisi, *Bihar Al-Anwar*, 81:244.
[24] Al-Subhani, *Sirat al-A' immah*, 519-520.

God protect you from all evil. We have no doubt that anyone who truly believed that his prayer is or is likely to be his last will put great passion in it and approach God with a pure heart, asking for mercy and forgiveness.

Our Holy Imams (a) have emphasized the need for having this mental state when approaching the prayer. This can surely create a feeling of reverence for God for a believer. As Imam Sadiq (a) is reported to have said,

> *If you perform an obligatory prayer, perform it at its set time and pray as if it is your last prayer. Be wary that you may not be able to perform a prayer again. Focus your gaze on your place of prostration. If you only knew who is to your right and who is to your left! Surely, you would have performed your prayer well. Know that you are in the presence of He who sees you while you cannot see Him.*[25]

*Devotion in Worship*

This is one of the most important steps for reaching a state of reverence for God. When a person clears his time and his mind of all tasks and worries but worship of God and approaches the prayer with devotion to God, only then will he be in a state of true supplication to God. The narrations have emphasized much on this issue, as it is a key step in reaching this state of reverence.

In one of our narrations, Imam Sadiq (a) clarifies for us how we can reach this level of devotion in our worship. He (a) says,

---

[25] Al-Majlisi, *Bihar Al-Anwar*, 81:233.

*When you face the Qibla,*[26] *forget about the world and everything in it. Forget about creation and all their worries. Empty your heart of any distraction that disturbs your focus on God. Contemplate in your heart the Grandeur of God. Remember that you will stand before Him on the day* 'every soul will examine what it has sent in advance, and they will be returned to God, their real master.'[27] *Stand on the peg of fear and hope. When you say 'Allahu Akbar' (God is Greatest), contemplate on the triviality of everything between the high heavens and the earth compared to His Greatness. If God the Exalted sees in the heart of a servant while he says Allahu Akbar a distraction from the reality of His Greatness, He will say, 'Oh liar! Do you think you can deceive Me? By My Honor and Majesty, I will deprive you of the sweetness of My remembrance. I will veil you [away] from My proximity and the pleasure of true supplication to Me.' Know that He is not in need of your service and He is needless of your worship and supplication. Rather, He called you [to worship Him] by His Grace so that He may have mercy on you, distance you from His punishment, shower you with the blessings of His Absolute Compassion, guide you to the path of His contentment, and open for you the doors of His forgiveness. Surely, if God the Exalted had created more than the number of the realms of His creation multiplied manifold in infinite eternity, it would still make no difference to Him whether they all disbelieved in Him or believed in His Oneness. He only has His creation worship Him in order to*

---

[26] Qibla is the direction of prayer. All Muslims pray towards one point on this Planet; the Kaaba in Mecca, modern day Saudi Arabia.

[27] The Holy Quran. Chapter 10 [Jonah; Arabic: *Younis*]. Verse 30.

> *show [His] Generosity and Ability. So take modesty [before Him] as your cloak and dependence [on Him] as your robe. Enter into the grandeur of God's dominion, and you will reap the benefits of His Lordship in your absolute dependence on Him and your Distress for Him.*[28]

.We should exert our efforts in attempting to reach the utmost level of devotion. This will allow us to reap the benefits of prayers. Else, we surely would be depriving ourselves of this great opportunity. It is very sad that when we turn to prayer and begin with its rituals, our minds begin to wander. We start to think of anything and everything but our prayers. That is truly a grave deprivation.

## The Prophet (s) and His Household (a)

All of this can be achieved if we go back to the life and teachings of the Prophet (s) and his Holy Household (a) and take them as examples and role models in our lives. Reading the traditions regarding reverence and devotion in prayers will bring us closer to grasping these realities.

If we were to look at their lives and see the great reverence that they showed in the prayers, we would see how trivial the prayers that we offer are. This should encourage us to improve our prayers so we can inch closer to them. If they lived in such a state of reverence, fear, and hope, we must all strive to reach that state. These emotions that boil within an individual are indicative of his relationship with God.

Let us mention a few examples from the life of the Prophet (s) and his Family (a) here.

---

[28] Al-Majlisi, *Bihar Al-Anwar*, 81:230.

PRACTICES

1. It is narrated that "when the Prophet (s) would stand for prayer, his face would change colors out of fear of God...."[29] It is also narrated that "when the Prophet (s) would get up to pray, he would be [in long prostration] like a piece of clothing thrown [on the ground]."[30]
2. It is also narrated that when the time of prayer came, the Commander of the Faithful (a) would tremble and change colors. When he was asked about this, he would say, *"The time has come for the Divine Trust that God offered to the heavens and the earth but they refused to carry it and were distressed from it. But mankind has carried it. [In my weakness,] I do not know whether I will do well in delivering [the trust] which I was charged with carrying or not."*[31]
3. It is narrated that Lady Fatima (a) used to be [out of breath] in her prayers due to fear of God.[32]
4. Imam Sadiq (a) narrates that when Imam Hasan (a) stood for prayer *"his limbs would tremble in the presence of his Exalted Lord. Whenever he would recall paradise and hellfire, he would quiver as if bit [by a snake], asking God for paradise and seeking refuge in God from hellfire."*[33]

And this is the case for all of our Immaculate Imams (a). May God make us all of those who are reverent in their prayers, and all praise be to God.

---

[29] Al-Majlisi, *Bihar Al-Anwar*, 81:248.
[30] Ibid.
[31] Ibid.
[32] Ibid, 81:258.
[33] Ibid.

# THE MOSQUE

*In the Name of God the Beneficent the Merciful*

*The places of worship belong to God, so do not invoke anyone along with God.*[1]

There is no doubt that building a house of worship for the sake of God is a great and blessed act of devotion. Such a pure place has great significance in the life of individual Muslims and the community as a whole. Through this place, the spirits of the believers ascend to the celestial realms. Through worship and remembrance of God, the individual achieves a level of harmony with all of creation. God says, *"The seven heavens glorify Him, and the earth [too], and whoever is in them. There is not a thing but celebrates His praise, but you do not understand their glorification. Indeed, He is all-forbearing, all-forgiving."*[2]

The mosque is a significant station in which this harmony is achieved, as the human being chooses with his free will to worship God Almighty along with the rest of creation. This may be why the Prophet (s) has emphasized the importance

---

[1] The Holy Quran. Chapter 72 [Arabic: *Al-Jinn*]. Verse 18.
[2] The Holy Quran. Chapter 17 [The Ascension; Arabic: *Al-Israa*]. Verse 44.

of building mosques – it is narrated that he said, *"whoever builds a mosque, even if like [the size of] the place a sandgrouse clears [to lay its eggs], God will build for him a home in paradise."*[3]

The Imams of the Holy Household (a) have emphasized the importance of building mosques no matter how small and simple they are. We find in the narrations an emphasis on building mosques by placing stones to demarcate small places as mosques. In one narration, a companion of Imam Sadiq (a) asks him about the small mosques built by the pilgrims on their way to Mecca. The Imam (a) said, *"… those are the best of mosques. Whoever builds a mosque like [the size of]*[4] *the place a sandgrouse clears [to lay its eggs], God will build for him a home in paradise."*[5]

## THE SIGNIFICANCE OF THE MOSQUE

Places on this Earth do not differ in nobility because of the place's relationship to someone who is noble. The nobler the being associated to the land, the nobler the land itself becomes. That is why we see that when a noble man – a prophet or a righteous servant – is buried in a plot of land, that land gains great status. It comes to hold great value for the followers of this noble personality and those who know of his status. The same happens when a noble individual takes a place as his home or place of worship, for instance. Think of the Temple Mount in Judaism, the tomb of Saint

---

[3] Al-Ihsaei, *'Awali Al-La'ali*, 2:30.

[4] The analogy of the sandgrouse in this tradition and the previous one may have more significance than simply the matter of size. For more, see Sayyid Jalal al-Din al-Husayni's footnote commentary on this tradition in al-Mahasin, as referenced below.

[5] Al-Barqi, *Al-Mahasin*, 1:55.

Peter in Catholicism, or the Mosque of the Prophet (s) in Islam.

It is from this perspective that mosques have a great value incomparable to any other land. They are particularly associated with God, and there is nothing nobler than God. No association is better than association with God. This gives mosques their sacredness and status, in addition to the evidence from the Holy Scripture and traditions that make this clear. Generally, nothing belonging to the mosque can be taken out of it to be used for other purposes. It is forbidden to make the mosque impure, or else it must be purified promptly.

God's compassion for His servants has dictated that houses of worship (mosques) be built where He is to be worshiped and where His servants can grow closer in proximity to Him. It is narrated that Imam Sadiq (a) said, *"Come to the mosques, for they are the houses of God on Earth. Whoever comes to them in purity God will purify him of his sins and consider him His guest. So frequent them for prayers and supplication...."*[6]

This is why great importance is put on the building of mosques. It is a means of connecting to God and an indication to the strength of that connection. However, God does not only want buildings, but wants mosques built on the principle of piety. As for mosques that were not built on piety, those are far from what God wants. This is why God instructed the Prophet (s) to avoid the mosques that were built on hypocrisy rather than piety. God says,

---

[6] Al-Sadouq, *Al-Amali*, 440.

*As for those who took to a mosque for sabotage and for defiance, and to cause division among the faithful, and for the purpose of ambush [used] by those who have fought God and His Apostle before—they will surely swear, 'We desired nothing but good,' and God bears witness that they are indeed liars. Do not stand in it ever! A mosque founded on God-wariness from the [very] first day is worthier that you stand in it [for prayer]. Therein are men who love to keep pure, and God loves those who keep pure. Is he who founds his building on God-wariness and [the pursuit of God's] pleasure better-off or he who founds his building on the brink of a collapsing bank which collapses with him into the fire of hell? God does not guide the wrongdoing lot.*[7]

So piety is an essential requirement for one establishing a house of worship.

## Mosques in our Daily Lives

Because mosques are houses of God and provide a connection to Him, they play a large role in the lives of the believers. A mosque plays a significant role in an individual's exemplification of true servitude to God.

### Worship

God Almighty created humans and jinn in order to worship Him. The entirety of creation revolves around this purpose. Through worship of the One and Only worthy of absolute devotion, an individual can become more deeply aware and conscious of the Greatest of All, God Almighty. That is a worthy goal in and of itself. In fact, there is perhaps no wor-

---

[7] The Holy Quran. Chapter 9 [Arabic: *Al-Tawba*]. Verses 107-09.

thier goal imaginable. God, the All-Generous, wants the best for His creatures and so He made worship the goal for His creation.

Sincere servitude to God Almighty forms a deep connection between the individual and God. Through such servitude, one can soar toward greater levels of excellence. True servitude to God means true freedom from all else. Only God the Almighty is worthy of such absolute servitude, as everything else is fading and temporary. None of His creations have any power or ability except those as granted by Him. One of the most evident manifestation of servitude is the act of prayer. If it is accepted, everything else is accepted. And if it is rejected, all else is rejected. It is the means of ascension for the pious. It is a journey towards God. The mosque is the designated place for this important worship. The rewards of praying in the mosque are emphasized by the Immaculate Ones (s). This does not come as a surprise, for the mosque is the place that was built for the purpose of prayer and other worships.

The same is true for supplication; an act that has been described as the "heart of worship." The mosque plays a large role in the realization of this worship as well. Supplication has a special place in a believer's life, as it achieves for him two things: it allows him to express his humility, need, and dependence on God; and it allows him to express his faith in the absolute self-sufficiency, power, and ability that God possesses. It is a very practical form of worship. Perhaps it is considered the heart of worship because it is a direct and practical admission of a human's dependence on God as well as a human's humility before God's power and authority. Supplicating to God is a worship and abandoning it is a form of arrogance – "*Your Lord has said, 'Call Me, and I will hear you!' Indeed those who are disdainful of My worship will enter hell in utter humiliation.*"[8] The scholars of exegesis tell us that worship in this verse refers primarily to supplications. God wants the best for us. Thus, He warns us to worship Him and not to harm ourselves with the conceit of neglecting supplications to God.

Mosques are said to be places where supplications and prayers are answered, as they are the houses of God and we are His guests in those houses. Our Immaculate Imams (a) have instructed us to hold fast to prayers and supplications in the mosque. Our Imams (a) have also taught us the great benefits of congregational prayers and supplications, as they are more rewarding and may be answered more readily.

*Seeking Knowledge*

Islam put great emphasis on seeking knowledge, as knowledge is one of things that actualize servitude and devotion to God. That is why God declares "*Only those of God's servants having knowledge fear Him.*"[9] In fact, seeking knowledge is regarded as one of the greatest forms of worship. God prefers people of knowledge over all others; "*Are those who know equal to those who do not know?*"[10]

Facilitating the pursuit of knowledge is the great role that mosques have played since the time of the Prophet (s), who himself instilled this concept in the fabric of the Muslim

---

[8] The Holy Quran. Chapter 40 [Arabic: *Ghafir*]. Verse 60.
[9] The Holy Quran. Chapter 35 [Arabic: *Fatir*]. Verse 28.
[10] The Holy Quran. Chapter 9 [Arabic: *Al-Zumar*]. Verse 9.

community. Our Immaculate Imams (a) followed this path, taking mosques as educational centers. Mosques became universities open to the public. Scholars of all sciences would use them as a place of learning and teachings, but that was especially true for Islamic sciences. Indeed, the Grand Mosque of the Prophet (s) was the first university in Islam, from which many scholars graduated. Mosques throughout the Muslim community played a similar role. The Grand Mosque of Kufa, for example, played an integral role in spreading the knowledge of the Holy Household (a). The Mosque of Al-Azhar in Egypt and the Mosque of Qarawiyyin in Morroco played similar roles. Mosques throughout the Muslim world educated thousands of scholars who became the vanguards of sciences through the decades.

Generally, mosques have never been places for empty worship, unenlightened by the beacons of knowledge that guide us on our journey towards God. For indeed, the Immaculate ones (s) teach us that the contemplation of an hour is better than staying up an entire night in worship [without contemplation]. This is why seeking useful knowledge is more worthy of one's effort than the monasticism of the ignorant. This is not to downplay the importance of recommended prayers, supplications, acts of charity, staying up at night to worship God, etc… However, the quality in such acts of devotion can be impacted profoundly by one's pursuit for useful knowledge and contemplation.

Therefore, mosques that do not carry the message of knowledge have been stripped of their true purpose. True worship is that which is combined with knowledge.

Knowledge lights the path of the individual towards God and allows him to avoid the traps of Satan. Spreading knowledge is one of the greatest objectives of the mosque and the noblest of its roles.

*Community Interactions*

The mosque also plays a large role in strengthening community interactions, a role that is highly emphasized in Islam. Islam regards the Muslim community as a single body; the Prophet (s) said *"the example of the believers in their affection, mercy, and compassion for each other is that of a single body. When any limb aches, the whole body reacts with sleeplessness and fever."*[11] The great importance that is placed on community interactions has at least two benefits:

**Strengthening a Sense of Belonging**. Our journey towards God is filled with struggle and strife. It is a path which Satan has filled with his traps. This is why we must journey in a caravan that is sure to take us towards God. This caravan must be filled with enough provisions for this long journey. And *"woe for the lack of provisions and the length of the journey."*[12] On this journey, we must always advise each other with virtue and patience.

From this perspective, one can imagine why there is a great emphasis on communal prayers and supplication as a community. When these worships are performed as a community, the believer does not feel that he is alone on this journey and he is thus less likely to stray. The believers support each

---

[11] Al-Hindi, *Kanz Al-'Ummal*, 1:149.
[12] Al-Radi, *Nahj Al-Balagha*, 18:224.

other on this path. It is narrated that the Commander of the Faithful (a) said,

> *Whoever comes to the mosque will attain one of eight things: a supportive brother on the path to God, novel knowledge, a clear verse [of the Quran], a mercy that is awaited [or awaiting], advice that dissuades him from wrong, hearing a word that leads him to guidance, or he would leave a sin due to fear or embarrassment.*[13]

**Preservation of the General Order.** Islam gives special attention to preserving the social order of the Muslim community. For example, in contracts and other dealings, just witnesses may be required to ensure as method of verifying the transaction. The Mosque plays a role in strengthening interactions between members of the community, and allows individuals to come to know the just and righteous among them. This is an important factor used to establish the credibility of witnesses and thus resolve disputes; matters which are integral to the preservation of social order. It has been reported that Imam Sadiq (a) said:

> *Indeed, [God] has made congregational prayers and [obligated] meeting for prayers so that [people] may know who prays and who does not pray, and who respects the times of prayers and who does not. Without this, no one would ever be able to testify as to the virtue of anyone else, because whoever does not pray the congregational prayers has no prayer among the Muslims [that they can testify to]. For, indeed, the Messenger of God (s) said, 'there is no prayer for whoev-*

---

[13] Al-Sadouq, *Al-Amali*, 474.

*er does not pray with the Muslims in the mosque except for an exigency.*[14]

Although congregational prayers are not obligatory, this is one narration in which the Imam (a) points to the importance of congregational prayers as an indicator of a Muslim's commitment to practicing the faith. According to this tradition, the Prophet (s) also describes the prayer with the Muslims in the mosque in such high regard that it is as if one who does not partake in it has not prayed, unless that person had a valid excuse.

## Purification of the Self

One of the first and major objectives of divine laws is to provide a mechanism for self-purification, and based on what we have previously discussed, we can see that the mosque plays a major role in this regard. We notice that simply meeting at any location for the purpose of worshipping God and seeking proximity to Him allows the souls to transcend worldly connections and ascend towards God. A person who postpones his social, economic, and other activities to perform a prayer in the mosque is attempting to grow closer to God. No power can force him to go to the Mosque and no law requires that he does. Rather, a person must have a personal drive that stems from his love for God to leave everything and head to the mosque. This person has great self-control so that he abandons his desires and heads towards the pleasure of God.

This is in addition to the divine connection that the mosque establishes, so that it comes to represent all the blessings of

---

[14] Al-Sadouq, *'Ilal Al-Sharae'*, 2:325.

God. This connection to God becomes the source of our personal virtue and strength on our journey. We gain mercy because of our association with the All-Merciful. We gain virtue because of our association with His absolute good. We also see that the mosque is a place for wisdom and advice, where the Muslims counsel and consult each other and support one another. All these are essential for self-purification. And the mosque plays a central role in all this, as the slogan of mosque-goers will be *"The places of worship belong to God, so do not invoke anyone along with God."*[15]

And as Imam Sadiq (a) said, *"Come to the mosques, for they are the houses of God on Earth. Whoever comes to them in purity God will purify him of his sins and consider him His guest. So frequent them for prayers and supplication...."*[16]

---

[15] The Holy Quran. Chapter 72 [Arabic: *Al-Jinn*]. Verse 18.
[16] Al-Sadouq, *Al-Amali*, 440.

# The Holy Quran

*In the Name of God the Beneficent the Merciful*

*God has sent down the best of discourses, a scripture [composed] of similar motifs, whereat shiver the skins of those who fear their Lord, then their skins and hearts relax at God's remembrance. That is God's guidance, by which He guides whomever He wishes; and whomever God leads astray, has no guide.*[1]

No two Muslims differ over the importance of the Holy Quran, as it is one of our core beliefs that it is the word of God. Every single verse in the Quran is from God, revealed to Prophet Muhammad (s). Generation after generation of Muslims have passed it down as it is today in an uninterrupted chain tracing back to the time of Prophet Muhammad (s). It is a miracle which has challenged the experts of its time and continues to challenge the experts of every age ever since. God is far too Wise and Kind than to have allowed for a miracle to aid a person with such a false claim, as it would misguide those who do not know any better. Thus, the Holy Quran is a testament to the truth of Prophet

---

[1] The Holy Quran. Chapter 39 [Arabic: *Al-Zumar*]. Verse 23.

Muhammad's (s) claims. Furthermore, everything in the Quran is true because it is from God Almighty; *"falsehood cannot approach it, at present or in future, a [revelation gradually] sent down from One all-wise, all-laudable."*[2]

It is the message that God has honored us with, and it will remain protected of all distortion; as God has promised, *"Indeed We have sent down the Reminder, and indeed We will preserve it."*[3] Because the original revealed scripture of other faiths have been altered or lost, we see a great deal of contradiction within their books. This unfortunately include many instances where God is mentioned in a way that is demeaning to His Glory or where some Prophets sent by God are mentioned in a way that is unbefitting of their impeccable character. These distortions have led many members of humanity away from the divine principles of faith even when they attempt to seek guidance in their holy scripture.

Despite the fact that the Quran has been protected by God from distortion, humanity will not be able to achieve righteousness and virtue if they, by their own will, disregard the Quran and its teachings.

## Relationship to the Quran

How do we assess our relationship to the Quran? Do we handle the Quran as only an object of ritual and custom? Or do we have a true connection with the words and meanings of the Holy Book?

---

[2] The Holy Quran. Chapter 41 [Arabic: *Fussilat*]. Verse 42.
[3] The Holy Quran. Chapter 15 [Arabic: *Al-Hijr*]. Verse 9.

In other words, is our relationship to the Quran limited to the ritual customs of kissing the book, displaying it at home, and holding on to it when we are sick? We do not reject these acts, rather we admit of the great benefits that they bring. But we must ask ourselves... is this the extent of our relationship to the Quran? Is this relationship enough for us to fulfill our duty towards the words of God? Or must the Quran be our guiding light in all aspects of our life? Is it enough to recite the Quran in the Holy Month of Ramadhan and at funerals? Or must we establish a connection with it through regular recitation?

The Quran does not need our kisses. It does not need us to place it on our heads and our hearts. The Quran calls for individuals to contemplate on and carry its meanings. It calls for individuals that will obey its command and restrain themselves from its prohibitions. Otherwise, we will be amongst those whom the Prophet (s) complains to God about because they have neglected the Quran. *"And the Apostle will say, 'O my Lord! Indeed my people consigned this Quran to oblivion.'"*[4]

## How to Establish a Relationship with the Quran

So we need to establish a strong relationship with the Quran and its meanings. How do we do that?

---

[4] The Holy Quran. Chapter 25 [Arabic: *Al-Furqan*]. Verse 30.

## Consistent Recitation

It is narrated that the Prophet (s) said, "*Safeguard your children through prayers [i.e. by teaching them prayers and all their obligations and etiquettes]. Teach them to do good, as doing good is a habit.*"[5] While this narration does not directly relate to our topic, it helps us understand our nature. It points out to us that we are very susceptible to formulating habits that will determine our path in life. Furthermore, habit is not a bad thing in and of itself, and can rather be used for our own growth and development.

If we connect the above-mentioned narration to our topic, we can deduce the following: that one of the main reasons for our weak relationship with the Quran is because we have not made recitation of its words a habit in our lives. We neglect to recite it throughout the year, and we only pick it during special occasions like the Holy Month of Ramadhan.

For us to create a deeper bond with the Quran, we must make it a habit to recite its verses. If we make it a habit to recite as little as two pages of the Quran a day, we will find that we will begin to miss the Quran and feel guilty about our neglect whenever we fail to recite it.

This is the first step in strengthening our relationship to the Quran. As we begin to taste the sweetness of recitation and the great blessings that it will bring, this relationship will grow stronger and stronger. We begin to realize these blessings when we read narrations such as the one of the Prophet (s) saying, "*If one of you loves to speak to his Lord, let him read

---

[5] Al-Bayhaqi, *Al-Sunan Al-Kubra*, 3:84.

*the Quran."*⁶ It is also narrated that the Prophet (s) once said, *"These hearts rust just as iron rusts."* When he was asked about how to remove this rust, he answered, *"Reciting the Quran."*⁷ These are only a couple of the many narrations that address the great benefits of recitation of the Holy Quran.

## Reflecting on its Meanings

After we make it a habit to recite the Holy Quran, we must take our relationship with it further by reflecting on the verses and their meanings. The more we think about, reflect on, and understand the Quran, the stronger our bond with it will become.

Some may think that the more pages of the Quran they read, the stronger their connection to it. Yes, dedicating time to read the Quran is good, but contemplating on its meanings is better. Reading the Quran without reflecting on its verses may not achieve for the individual the goals for which the Quran was revealed. The Quran was revealed to be understood and abided by. Reflecting on the verses – with reference to simple expositions by learned scholars – can give recitation of the Quran new meaning. This will strengthen the individual's bond with the Quran. It is narrated that the Prophet (s) said,

> *Oh Mo'ad! If you want the living of the fortunate, the death of martyrs, salvation on the Day of Resurrection, safety on the Day of Fear, light on the Day of Darkness, shade on the Day of Torrid Heat, satiation on the Day of Thirst, weight on the Day [on which one's deeds are] Light-*

---

⁶ Al-Reyshahri, *Mizan Al-Hikma*, 8:16197. Citing: Al-Hindi, *Kanz Al-'Ummal*, 2257.

⁷ Ibid, 8:16198. Citing: Ibn Abi Al-Hadid, *Sharh' Nahj Al-Balagha*, 2:23.

> *weighted [on the scale of deeds], and guidance on the Day of Deviance, then study the Quran. For it is surely a remembrance of the All-Merciful One, a protection against Satan, and a [factor] tipping the scales [of judgment to the side of salvation].*[8]

Of course, lack of mastery of the Arabic language is an enormous impediment to direct access to the Quran. Some may not read a word of Arabic. This is not to be mistaken as being an issue restricted to certain ethnicities or geographic areas. Even Muslims who were born in the Middle East and have spoken modern-day Arabic all their lives find difficulty in understanding the bare language of the Quran directly, let alone the deeper meanings. This is not because the language of the Quran is impossibly difficult to understand. Rather, we find that Muslims – whether Arab or not – will focus their efforts on learning and mastering foreign languages instead of focusing on mastering the language of the Quran. If we look at the lens in which people view language, it is not surprising to see that many do not understand the language of the Quran. Families prioritize learning of the languages they think are beneficial to their children's materialistic future, and neglect to teach them the language of their faith's Divine book.

Even with direct access to the bare language of the Quran, studying the Quran's deeper meanings and implications is an expertise requiring scholarship. Hence, non-expert access to understanding the Quran must be through scholarly exegesis. Furthermore, only the Holy Prophet (s) and our Im-

---

[8] Al-Reyshahri, *Mizan Al-Hikma*, 3: 2521. Citing: Al-Hindi, *Kanz Al-'Ummal*, 1:545.

maculate Imams (a) have a true and full understanding of the Quran's deepest meanings. Therefore, the only way for us to gain a well-grounded understanding of the Holy Quran is through reference to the exegeses written by the expert scholars following the path of Ahl al-Bayt (a).

We should also point out that translations of the Holy Quran do not do justice to its meanings. Many translations are inaccurate. All translations provide what the translator understands the verses to convey, and that understanding is often debatable and sometimes inconsistent with the principles of our faith. The available translations can, however, be used as a guide to gaining a general understanding of what a verse may mean, but it cannot provide a precise and accurate enough translation to another language.

Ideally, to best understand the meanings of the Quran and form a greater bond with it, we should read it in the language that it was revealed. Furthermore, if we can, we should gain expert insight into the exegesis ourselves through proper training, or at least refer to the experts for the appropriate exegesis and commentary. One cannot seek comfort and learning from reading a text that one does not understand. Therefore, we should focus on learning the Arabic language in order to be able to connect with the Quran on a deeper level.

## *Memorizing its Verses*

One of the important means to strengthening the individual's connection to the Holy Quran comes through memorization of its verses. When a person memorizes the verses of the Quran, these verses will accompany him at all times. We may not at all times be able to pick up a hard copy of the

Quran and recite its verses. We may not be able to read it from a hard copy while we walk, drive, shop, etc. However, if we have memorized verses of the Quran, we can recollect them at all times. These verses begin to take root deep inside the individual's heart and soul. The verses can have a real effect on the character of the individual. If the person knows the true value of these words of God, and applies them truly, he will become through this a walking example of the Quran both in speech and in action. Whenever he crosses an opportunity to do good, he will recollect the verses that will drive him towards it. Whenever he crosses an opportunity to deviate, he will recollect the verses that will drive him to avert it. In this regard, a person who has memorized the Quran may begin to live in harmony with its teachings and may better manifest these verses in his actions. This is why we put great emphasis on memorization of the Quran's verses – as it is narrated that the Prophet (s) said, *"whomever God has granted him memorization of His book, but thinks that someone else has been granted better than he has been granted, has been ungrateful of the best of blessings."*[9] The Prophet (s) is also narrated to have said *"whoever does not have in him some part of the Quran [i.e. memorized some of its verses] is [empty] like a ruined home."*[10]

Memorization of the Quran requires constant recollection. If a person memorizes a verse but does not actively recollect it, he may soon forget it. It is narrated that the Prophet (s) said, *"Look after the Quran [with frequent care]. For it is un-*

---

[9] Al-Reyshahri, *Mizan Al-Hikma*, 3:2522. Citing: Al-Hindi, *Kanz Al-'Ummal*, 1:518.
[10] Ibid. Citing: Al-Hindi, *Kanz Al-'Ummal*, 1:553.

*tamed... it is quicker to escape the hearts of men than the camels that escape their binds....*"[11]

When a person learns of the effects of forgetting anything that he had memorized of the Holy Quran, it will drive him to constant reading and recollection of the verses. It is narrated that Imam Sadiq (a) said,

> *Whenever a person forgets a chapter of the Quran, it will be manifested for him in a beautiful shape and a high status in Paradise. When he sees it he will ask 'who are you? You're so beautiful? I wish you were mine.' It will reply, 'do you not know me? I am such and such chapter [of the Quran], and had you not forgotten me, I would have elevated you with me to this status."*[12]

Of course, the essential goal of memorizing the Quran is to facilitate a reminder of its verses, the proper understanding of those verses and the appropriate application of those verses in one's life. Surely, the benefit of merely memorizing without understanding or practicing pales – if it exists – in comparison to the benefit of memorizing, understanding and practicing the teachings of the Quran.

*Listening to its Words*

Another of the important means for strengthening the relationship with the Holy Quran is to listen to its words. Of course, we must point out the significance of reading the Quran, as it has its many rewards and benefits, and plays a large role in strengthening this relationship. However, listening to the Quran can also play an important role. This may

---

[11] Ibid, 3:2523. Citing: Al-Hindi, *Kanz Al-'Ummal*, 1:618.
[12] Ibid. Citing: Al-Amili, *Wasael Al-Shia*, 4:845.

go back to the fact that recitation requires heavy dependence on the person's vision, whereas listening to the Quran involves other senses in a fundamental way. And sometimes listening to the words of the Quran can have a greater spiritual impact on the individual. In fact, this may be why the Quran points out the link between listening to its words and increased spirituality,

> *Say, 'Whether you believe in it, or do not believe in it, indeed when it is recited to those who were given knowledge before it, they fall down in prostration on their faces,' and say, 'Immaculate is our Lord! Indeed Our Lord's promise is bound to be fulfilled. Weeping, they fall down on their faces, and it increases them in humility.'*[13]

It is possible that a person may recite the Quran and not pay close attention to its words, as he may be preoccupied with correct articulation of the words and recitation of the verses. This may preoccupy his mind from contemplation and spirituality. Whereas, when a person listens to the Quran and directs himself fully to it, his mind may be more open for its words, allowing for greater contemplation and spirituality. However, this is only a possibility that we suggest here. It's not necessarily true in all or even most cases, especially if the reciter listens carefully to what he is reciting. But it could also be that recitation and listening to the words of God complement each other in achieving the Quran's purpose. There's a beautiful narration in this regard attributed to the Prophet (s) – *"The tribulations of this life are*

---

[13] The Holy Quran. Chapter 17 [The Ascension; Arabic: *Al-Israa*]. Verses 107-09.

*driven away from the reciter of the Quran. The tribulations of the hereafter are driven away from the listener to the Quran.*"[14]

Through proper application of these means a person can build a greater relationship with the Holy Quran. This sincere relationship is of utmost importance because it will lead one to the path of happiness. The Quran is the guide that will lead only to the better path.

---

[14] Al-Reyshahri, *Mizan Al-Hikma*, 3:2531. Citing: Al-Hindi, *Kanz Al-'Ummal*, 2:291.

# Supplication

*In the Name of God the Beneficent the Merciful*

*When My servants ask you about Me, [tell them that] I am indeed nearmost. I answer the supplicant's call when he calls Me. So let them respond to Me, and let them have faith in Me, so that they may fare rightly.*[1]

There are times during the year, like the Month of Ramadan, that God created out of his generosity, mercy and favor for his servants. *"And God would not let your prayers go to waste. Indeed God is most kind and merciful to mankind."*[2] These times of the year play a fundamental role in rejuvenating the human spirit and bringing us closer to our Creator. These 'spiritual seasons' stimulate our hearts and minds, taking us out of our worldly routines to direct us back to God and our purpose. The sinner will turn to his Lord in repentance and the good-doer will turn to God asking for more blessing and guidance to help him continue in serving God. No matter what state a person is in, if he seeks to benefit from these seasons he will be a winner. If he neglects these mo-

---

[1] The Holy Quran. Chapter 2 [The Cow; Arabic: *Al-Baqara*]. Verse 186.
[2] The Holy Quran. Chapter 2 [The Cow; Arabic: *Al-Baqara*]. Verse 143.

ments of opportunity, he will be at a loss. All in all, God is unaffected by whether we turn to Him or not – it is solely to our benefit or detriment. Whether it is in the months of Rajab, Shaaban, or Ramadan, we can't stress enough how important it is to take advantage of these blessed times to seek closeness to God.

## THE ROLE OF SUPPLICATION IN WORSHIP

Especially during those three months, there are numerous acts of worship that are highly recommended in seeking closeness to God. You can find many of these recommended acts in books like *Mafateeh Al-Jinan* by Sheikh Abbas Al-Qummi. According to some traditions attributed to the Holy Prophet (s) and Ahlulbayt (a), supplication is the best of worship. Imam Al-Baqir (a) said, *"God says, 'Call Me, and I will hear you!' Indeed those who are disdainful of My worship will enter hell in utter humiliation."*[3] *That is supplication, and the best of worship is supplication…"*[4] Imam Al-Baqir (a) was asked, "Which is better: increased reading [of the Quran] or increased supplication?" The Imam (a) responded, *"Supplication. Have you not heard the words of God, 'Say, 'Were it not for the sake of summoning you [to faith], what store my Lord would have set by you?'"*[5],[6]

According to tradition, the Holy Prophet (s) considered supplication to be the heart of worship. It is narrated that he has said, *"Supplication [to God] is [sheer worship]. One with suppli-*

---

[3] The Holy Quran. Chapter 40 [Arabic: *Ghafir*]. Verse 60.
[4] Al-Kulayni, *Al-Kafi*, 2:466.
[5] The Holy Quran. Chapter 25 [Arabic: *Al-Furqan*]. Verse 77.
[6] Al-Majlisi, *Bihar Al-Anwar*, 90:299.

*cation [to God] is not destroyed.*"[7] This narration and the others like it illustrate to us the grand importance of supplication and its role in worshipping God.

## WHEN SUPPLICATION IS NOT ANSWERED

Some pose the question: if supplication is so important in worship whereby there are verses in the Quran guaranteeing that the supplicant's prayers will be answered then why is it that sometimes our supplications are not answered?

Before answering this question it's important to make something very clear. God fulfills His promises. So, if we see a deficiency of some kind in the fulfillment of an expectation we have it is not because of God; rather, the deficiency is our own. We tend to blame things on others, even God, when things don't go our way, instead of claiming responsibility and contemplating what we can be doing differently. Nonetheless, it is important for us to discuss two essential points: the requirements of our supplications being answered and the barriers that hinder our supplications from being answered. It goes without saying that we should understand what elements we need to fulfill so that we can have our supplications answered. Likewise, we should be aware of what may stand in the way of having our supplications answered.

---

[7] Ibid, 90:300.

# When are Supplications Answered?

## Knowledge

One of the most essential factors in ensuring that supplications are answered is the supplicant's knowledge of God. Someone who is ignorant of God does not value Him nor can he be sincere in his supplication to God. Sincerity in supplication comes through knowledge and awareness of God. The more knowledge and awareness a person has, the more sincere his supplication can be and the more focused he can be on the one he supplicates to. Notice how people frequently ask pious scholars to make a special prayer or supplication to God for them. The supplications of the pious scholars, the vicegerents, and the prophets are considered to be ones that are not rejected; and thus, people seek them out for their supplications. The greater a person's awareness of God is the more likely his supplication will be answered.

Some people came up to Imam Al-Sadiq (a) and said, "*We supplicate but we are not answered.*" The Imam (a) replied, "*That is because you supplicate to one you do not know.*"[8] It is also narrated that Imam Al-Sadiq (a) said,

> *If a servant supplicated to God with a pure intention and a sincere heart, he will be answered after having fulfilled God's covenant. If, however, he supplicated to God without [pure] intention and sincerity then he will not be answered. Doesn't God say, 'and fulfill My covenant that I may fulfill your covenant,'[9]...* [10]

---

[8] Al-Sadouq, *Al-Tawheed*, 289.
[9] The Holy Quran. Chapter 2 [The Cow; Arabic: *Al-Baqara*]. Verse 40.

## Honest Living

Another fundamental element that has a substantial effect on the life of a believer is his livelihood. The type of work you do to put food on the table could be a reason for the answer or rejection of your supplications and prayers. The Holy Prophet (s) said, *"Whoever wants his supplications answered should make sure he has an honest living and means of sustenance."*[11] It is also narrated that the Prophet (s) said, *"Make your way of living honest and your supplications will be answered. If a man is to eat from what is forbidden his prayers will not be answered for forty days."*[12]

## Presence of Heart

True supplication comes from the heart. If our hearts remain in a state of heedlessness and forgetfulness then our supplications will be nothing more than words that are said. Why should we expect God to answer our supplication when they don't come from our hearts? God knows everything, He knows what is in each and every one of us. He knows who is sincere and who is fake, who is focused and who is distracted, who is honest and who is lying. Apply this between human beings for example. You go up to your friend asking for a favor. You really want them to help you. As you approach he stands there anticipating you and carefully listens to what you are about to say. Instead of reciprocating that attention, you ask him for the favor while you're texting, eating, or doing something else. You're barely looking at your friend or paying attention to him as you ask.

---

[10] Al-Majlisi, *Bihar Al-Anwar*, 90:379.
[11] Ibid, 90:372.
[12] Ibid, 90:358.

Would you blame him for not helping you? Any reasonable person would blame himself or herself for not having the bare minimum of proper etiquette in asking for a favor. The same applies to our supplication to God, and at a much higher degree. But God wants us to observe proper etiquette for our own good, not for His own personal benefit. He wants us to be the best that we can be. He wants us to strive for excellence and deeper awareness of the Greatest of all, God Himself. That is a goal worthy in and of itself. God is not in need of us, we are in dire need of Him. If our hearts do not become humble before Him and focus completely on Him, we are missing the point. The Prophet (s) said, *"God does not accept the supplication of one whose heart is oblivious."*[13] He also said, *"Know that God will not accept the supplication that comes from a heedless heart."*[14]

## BARRIERS TO SUPPLICATION

Just as there are requirements for being answered in supplication, there are also barriers to being answered. Our supplications may be in the right condition to be answered, but some barriers may come in the way to prevent it. Those barriers include the following:

### Sin

Our sins can stand in the way of our supplications being answered. Sinning may also be an indication of lack of proper knowledge or awareness of God. Thus, the supplications taught to us by Ahlulbayt (a) sometimes include the

---

[13] Al-Sadouq, *Man La Yahdaruh Al-Faqih*, 4:367.
[14] Al-Majlis, *Bihar Al-Anwar*, 74:173.

following prayer: "*O' God, forgive me those sins that hold back supplication...*"[15] Sins are veils and barriers to supplication. It is narrated that Imam Al-Baqir (a) said,

> *A servant asks God for his need, and thus God will grant him in a short period of time. The servant then sins. God then says to his angel: 'Do not fulfill his need, forbid him from it. He has exposed himself to My wrath and mandated deprivation [for himself] from me.*[16]

There are specific sins that deprive us of having our supplications answered, as narrated by the Ahlulbayt (a). It is reported that Imam Ali Zain Al-Abideen (a) said,

> *The sins which turn away one's supplications are: ill intention, hidden decadence, hypocrisy with one's brethren, forsaking belief that God will answer one's supplications, delaying one's mandatory prayers until their time has passed, and giving up getting closer to God Almighty through righteousness and charity...*[17]

## Oppression

When a person oppresses, God forbids an answer to his prayer. Oppressors are very far from the mercy of God, and thus their supplications are not answered. It is enough to mention the following narration of the Commander of the Faithful (a): "*God advised Jesus (a) the son of Mary (a): say to the chiefs of the children of Israel... I will not answer a supplication to any one of you who is oppressive to another from my creation.*"[18]

---

[15] Al-Tusi, *Misbah Al-Mutahajjid*, 844.
[16] Al-Kulayni, *Al-Kafi*, 2:361.
[17] Al-Huwayzi, *Nour Al-Thaqalayn*, 4:534.
[18] Al-Sadouq, *Al-Khisal*, 337.

## *Contradicting Divine Wisdom*

At times God does not answer the supplication of His servants because such a supplication conflicts with His divine wisdom. If divine wisdom dictates that a person remains poor, because in that materialistic poverty that person will see true happiness, God will not answer his supplication to become wealthy. Indeed, sometimes if a person becomes wealthy in terms of materialistic gains it can be a cause for the person's misery and misguidance, God forbid. The grace of God reins in ensuring that only the best happens for the person. God's kindness and generosity could actually be found in not answering a person's supplication because that specific supplication is not the best thing for him: *"Yet it may be that you dislike something, which is good for you, and it may be that you love something, which is bad for you, and God knows and you do not know."*[19]

---

[19] The Holy Quran. Chapter 2 [The Cow; Arabic: *Al-Baqara*]. Verse 216.

# SALAWAT

*In the Name of God the Beneficent the Merciful*

*Indeed God and His angels bless the Prophet; O you who have faith! Invoke blessings on him and invoke Peace upon him in a worthy manner.*[1]

In the special season of worship, being the three holy months of Rajab, Sha'ban, and Ramadan, there are a number of acts that illuminate the soul and bring us closer to our Creator. Of the many acts of worship that have been emphasized in our traditions, one particular act stands out – 'salawat'. Salawat is a reference to asking God to shower blessings upon our Holy Prophet Muhammad (s) and his Household (a). Imam Zein Al-Abideen (a) eloquently asks God to shower blessings upon his great-grandfather the Prophet (s) in his daily prayer; an excerpt of the prayer reads, *"God shower your blessings upon Muhammad and his Household, the tree of Prophethood, the holders of the Message, the hosts of God's angels, the essence of knowledge, the Household of revelation..."*[2]

---

[1] The Holy Quran. Chapter 33 [The Parties; Arabic: *Al-Ahzab*]. Verse 56.
[2] Ibn Tawoos, *Iqbal Al-A'mal*, 3:300.

## Why Emphasize the Salutation?

The Holy Scripture puts great emphasis on this blessed prayer; truly one of the best of supplications and the greatest of acts. We realize how great this act is when we speak of its consequences and benefits. We can summarize some of them in the following:

*Connecting to the Prophet*

Emphasis on sending salutations and invoking blessings upon the Prophet (s) and his Holy Household (a) is to strengthen the bond and connection that we have with our Grand Prophet (s). This invocation is one of the greatest manifestations of our bond with our Prophet (s) and one of the best means to strengthen it. Islam emphasizes the need to establish an emotional bond to the Prophet (s) and his Holy Household (a), as well as the intellectual and religious bond that we have through our faith. Faith cannot be complete without love and attachment to them. It is enough to note that the reward that we are compelled to pay the Prophet (s) for all his guidance and blessings is love for his family; "*Say, 'I do not ask you any reward for it except the love of [my] relatives.' Whoever performs a good deed, We shall enhance its goodness for him. Indeed God is all-forgiving, all-appreciative.*"[3]

It is not enough for a person to call himself a Muslim without creating a spiritual and emotional bond with the Prophet (s). That is because this bond plays its role in allowing us to follow his example and obey his commands. This salutation and invocation of blessings for the Prophet (s) is a matter agreed upon by the entire Muslim community. For it is a

---

[3] The Holy Quran. Chapter 42 [The Counsel; Arabic: *Al-Shura*]. Verse 23.

divine obligation stated in the Quran. "*Indeed God and His angels bless the Prophet; O you who have faith! Invoke blessings on him and invoke Peace upon him in a worthy manner.*"[4]

## The Prophet is the Path

The emphasis on sending salutations to the Prophet (s) and invoking God's blessings upon him is an indication that the path to God is by taking the example of the Grand Prophet (s) and the Immaculate Imams (a). There are countless claims out there about the path that can be taken to God. Yet the only rationally proven, scripturally verifiable path to Him is through the Prophet (s) and his Holy Household (a). The path to God is the path of truth. Truth stands alone in the face of falsehood, no matter how many forms falsehood takes. God has called upon us to take His path and leave all others. "*This indeed is my straight path, so follow it, and do not follow [other] ways, for they will separate you from His way. This is what He enjoins upon you so that you may be God-wary.*"[5]

An individual with access to the truth cannot receive the full extent of God's blessings if he does not fill his heart with the light of the Prophet (s). A heart that is empty of the Prophet's (s) light is not fit to be a vessel of God's greatest blessings. A narration of the Prophet (s) alludes to this; "*A person will not enter hellfire if he invokes blessings upon me. Whoever forgets to invoke blessings upon me has mistaken the way to paradise.*"[6]

---

[4] The Holy Quran. Chapter 33 [The Parties; Arabic: *Al-Ahzab*]. Verse 56.
[5] The Holy Quran. Chapter 6 [The Cattle; Arabic: *Al-An'aam*]. Verse 153.
[6] Al-Borojourdi, *Jami' Ahadeeth Al-Shia*, 15:463.

Therefore, the 'salawat' is a means to remain steadfast on the path of paradise. The path of paradise is the path of God. Neglecting to recite 'salawat' is straying away from the path of God.

A number of narrations state that sending these salutations and blessings will grant enlightenment of the heart. This will in turn guide the individual to the truth and allow him the ability to receive greater divine blessings. In a narration of Imam Rida (a), he says, *"The heart of a man is in a vessel covered with a lid. If a person [in that state] invokes blessings upon Muhammad (s) and the Household of Muhammad (a), a complete invocation, then the lid will be lifted and the heart will be enlightened..."*[7]

Our great scholar Allama Majlisi (ra) commented on this narration, saying

> *It is not far-fetched to believe that this narration [employs] metaphor and imagery. Invocation of blessings upon the Prophet (s) and his Holy Household (a) is a means to bring the individual closer to God and prepares the self to receive knowledge. It is as if the distractions [of this world] which create distance from God, the Exalted, are like a lid on [the vessel of] the self. Invocation of praise and blessings is a cause for removing this lid so that the heart is enlightened and ready to receive God's blessings....*[8]

This verifies what we mentioned earlier that 'salawat' is a means to enlighten the hearts and prepare it to receive divine blessings.

---

[7] Al-Majlisi, *Bihar Al-Anwar*, 91:51. Citing: Al-Sadouq, *'Oyun Akhbar Al-Rida*, 1:66.

[8] Al-Majlisi, *Mir' at al-'Uqul*, 6:204.

## *Salawat as Supplication*

Invocation of blessings upon the Prophet (s) is a supplication, asking God the Exalted to bless the Prophet (s) and his Family (a) and to raise their status and increase their proximity to Him. However, the benefits of this supplication essentially go back to the individual invoking it. Asking for the elevation of the status of the Prophet (s) is a supplication for greater blessings on the entire human race and all of creation. After all, God tells the Prophet (s) *"We did not send you but as a mercy to all the nations."*[9] Therefore, with the elevation of status of the Prophet (s) and his Family (a) comes a more profound blessing and a more intense mercy for all creation.

God blesses the Prophet (s) and commands His angels and mankind to pray and invoke His blessings for the Prophet (s). This brings great blessings to humanity as a whole.

This is again evident in the narration of Imam Sadiq (a) where he teaches us about the invocation of blessings upon the Prophet (s):

> *Oh my God! Muhammad (s) is just as You described him in Your book when You said,* 'There has certainly come to you an apostle from among yourselves. Grievous to him is your distress; he has deep concern for you, and is most kind and merciful to the faithful.'[10] *I bear witness that he was so, and that You did not command [mankind] to invoke blessings upon him until You Yourself and Your angels blessed him; as You said in*

---

[9] The Holy Quran. Chapter 21 [The Prophets; Arabic: *Al-Anbiyaa'*]. Verse 107.
[10] The Holy Quran. Chapter 9 [The Repentence; Arabic: *Al-Tawba*]. Verse 128.

*Your definitive Quran* 'Indeed God and His angels bless the Prophet; O you who have faith! Invoke blessings on him and invoke Peace upon him in a worthy manner.*[11]* *Not that there is any need for any of your creation to invoke blessings upon him after You have blessed him. Nor any need for them to praise him after You have praised him. Rather, all of creation are in need for that, as you have made him Your gate and you will not accept from anyone who comes to You except through [that gate]. You made invocation of blessings on him [cause] proximity to You, a means towards You, and a nearness to You. You guided the believers to him and commanded them to invoke your blessings upon him so that they increase in status [in Your eyes] and honor [in Your presence]. You assigned for those who invoke blessings upon him angels that invoke blessings on him and deliver to him [the believers'] invocation of blessings and salutations.[12]*

God is the one who raises the status of the Prophet (s), not us. We are the ones in need of the Prophet (s). All we can possibly do is what's in our own best interest: obey God's command, asking Him to raise the status of the Prophet (s) and his family. Therefore, invocation of praise and blessings on the Prophet (s) is primarily a blessing for the individual that undertakes it.

---

[11] The Holy Quran. Chapter 33 [The Parties; Arabic: *Al-Ahzab*]. Verse 56.
[12] Al-Majlisi, *Bihar Al-Anwar*, 87:82.

## The Meaning of Salawat

The meaning of 'salawat' may be clear to the reader by now, but there is no harm in returning to the narrations as a way of expanding upon that meaning.

It is narrated that Imam Sadiq (a) was asked about the verse *"Indeed God and His angels bless the Prophet; O you who have faith! Invoke blessings on him...."*[13] He answered, *"the blessings of God are a mercy, the blessings of His angels are praise, and the blessings of mankind are supplications..."*[14]

A number of our scholars have said,

> *Invocation of blessings means an invocation of mercy, but is used here to express the honor of the Prophet (s) and his great stature. 'Salat' can mean glorification, and it is said that [the invocation of salawat is of that type], meaning 'oh God, increase his honor in this world by raising his remembrance, expanding his message, and safeguarding his laws. And [increase his honor] in the next by allowing him intercession for his nation and increasing his rewards.*[15]

In any case, the holy verse that indicates that God blesses the Prophet (s) and so do His angels, and commands the believers to invoke that blessing, is a clear indication to the honor of the Prophet (s) and his stature in proximity to God. We should pause and contemplate on his character and honor.

---

[13] The Holy Quran. Chapter 33 [The Parties; Arabic: *Al-Ahzab*]. Verse 56.
[14] Al-Amili, *Wasael Al-Shia*, 4:1213.
[15] Al-Tabari, *Nawadir Al-Mo'jizat*, 68.

## The Method of Invoking Salawat

It is narrated, even by Sunni sources, that when the Prophet (s) was asked by his followers how they should invoke blessings upon him, he answered,

> *Say, 'Oh my God! Bless Muhammad and the Family of Muhammad just as You blessed Abraham and the Family of Abraham, You are Praiseworthy and Majestic. Oh my God! Honor Muhammad and the Family of Muhammad just as You honored Abraham and the Family of Abraham, You are Praiseworthy and Majestic.*[16]

"The author of Al-Dur Al-Manthoor listed eighteen other narrations in addition to this one, all of which explicitly state the necessity of mentioning the Family of Muhammad (a) during the invocation."[17]

Rather, all of the narrations that teach us how to invoke God's blessings upon the Prophet (s) include the Prophet's Holy Household (a). But it is really unfortunate that many Muslims do not mention the Holy Household (a), despite the Prophet's (s) explicit words against that. It is narrated that the Prophet (s) said *"do not invoke upon me a maimed invocation."* When he was asked about this, he answered, *"[Do not] say 'Oh my God! Bless Muhammad' and stop [there]. Rather, say 'Oh my God! Bless Muhammad and the Household of Muhammad.'"*[18]

---

[16] Al-Bukhari, *Sahih Bukhari*, 6:27.
[17] Al-Shirazi, *Al-Amthal*, 13:342.
[18] Ibn Hajar, *Al-Sawa'eq Al-Muhriqa*, 144.

## The Benefits of Salawat

Invocation of praise, salutations, and blessings on the Prophet (s) carry many benefits. Furthermore, those blessings are uncountable. Some of its blessings have a direct worldly effect, as well as the effects of the hereafter. We will briefly mention some of the most important here.

It is narrated that Imam Baqir (a) reported that Imam Sadiq (a) had said,

> *There is nothing in the balances [of deeds] more weighty than the invocation of blessings upon the Prophet (s) and his Household (a). A man's deeds would be placed on the scales and it would lean one way. Then he would take out his invocation of blessings upon the Prophet (s) and place it on the scales and it will lean the other way.*[19]

It is also narrated that the Prophet (s) said, "*I will stand at the scales on the Day of Resurrection. Whoever's sins outweigh his virtues, I will come with his invocation of blessings upon me so as to add weight to his virtues.*"[20]

It plays a role in permitting allowing the answering of our supplications. Imam Sadiq (a) is reported to have said, "*a supplication is blocked until [it is followed by] an invocation of blessings upon Muhammad and the Household of Muhammad.*"[21]

It plays a role in erasing misdeeds. It is narrated that Imam Rida (a) said, "*whoever is not able to find what will atone for his*

---

[19] Al-Borojourdi, *Jami' Ahadeeth Al-Shia*, 15:462.
[20] Ibid.
[21] Al-Majlisi, *Bihar Al-Anwar*, 87:155.

*sins, let him intensify his invocation of blessings upon Muhammad and the Household of Muhammad, as it surely annihilates sins."*[22]

It plays a role in cleansing the heart of hypocrisy. It is narrated that the Prophet (s) said, *"invocation of blessings upon me and my Household clears [the heart] of hypocrisy."*[23] It is also narrated that Imam Sadiq (a) narrated the following from the Prophet (s), *"raise your voices in invoking God's blessings upon me, as it clears [the heart] of hypocrisy."*[24]

Finally, it plays a large role in elevating an individual's status. It is narrated that Imam Sadiq (a) said,

> *If the Prophet (s) is mentioned, intensify your invocation of blessings upon him. Whoever invokes blessings upon the Prophet (s) once, God will bless him a thousand times followed by a thousand rows of angels. There will be no creation of God that would not invoke blessings upon this servant because of the blessings of God and His angels upon [this servant]. Whoever does not want this is an arrogant fool, and God, His Prophet (s), and the Household of the Prophet (a) renounce him.*[25]

---

[22] Al-Amili, *Wasael Al-Shia*, 4:1212.
[23] Al-Kulayni, *Al-Kafi*, 2:492.
[24] Al-Amili, *Wasael Al-Shia*, 4:1211.
[25] Ibid.

# FASTING

*In the Name of God the Beneficent the Merciful*

*O you who have faith! Prescribed for you is fasting as it was prescribed for those who were before you, so that you may be God-wary.*[1]

## WHY FAST?

The blessings that God has given us cannot be fully encompassed by our comprehension. *"If you enumerate God's blessings, you will not be able to count them."*[2] One of the most evident of these blessings for the believers is the blessing of being able to perform the obligatory fast. Although fasting may appear to be full of pain and suffering for the individual, it is in fact a great blessing and mercy to the believers.

However, the problem lies in that we judge everything with our defective materialistic notions, not by God's divine standards. This is where the Prophet (s) and his Holy Household (a) play their role to guide our attention towards

---

[1] The Holy Quran. Chapter 2 [The Cow; Arabic: *Al-Baqara*]. Verse 183.
[2] The Holy Quran. Chapter 14 [Abraham; Arabic: *Ibrahim*]. Verse 34.

the abundance of blessings and benefits in that great act. Still, many of us do not benefit from these blessings simply because we don't spend the time to learn about the importance of such worship. The Prophet (s) and the Immaculate Imams (a) have given us an abundance of narrations describing the benefits of these worships, and our grand scholars have meticulously collected, categorized, and explained these narrations. All that is left is for someone to go back to these books and review this great knowledge that we have been given. Once we go back and read these narrations, we can develop a better relationship with these worships and begin to elevate in spirituality. And that is not a hard thing to understand, as a person with more knowledge of a specific act will likely perform it better and excel at it. It is narrated that Imam Rida (a) said,

> *If it was asked, 'why were they commanded to fast?' then the answer would be 'so that they come to know the pain of hunger and thirst and infer from that [the severity of] the poverty of the hereafter. And so the person who is fasting becomes reverent, humble, servile, rewarded, saving [his reward to come from God for his sacrifice], realizing [of God's majesty], and patient over what has struck him of hunger and thirst so that he can deserve a reward [from God] for what he has undergone of refraining from desires. And so that [fasting] can become an admonishment for them in the short-term, a training for them to fulfil what God has obligated upon them, and a guide for them in the long-term. And so that they come to know the severity of what strikes*

*the poor and destitute in this world, so they give them what God has obligated [as alms] from their wealth....*[3]

This narration refers to some of the most important aspects of fasting. It does not list all of its benefits, as more benefits are listed in other narrations.

## POVERTY OF THE HEREAFTER

Mankind is created to live eternally in the hereafter, and this life is but a distraction. God says, "*The life of this world is nothing but diversion and play, but the abode of the Hereafter is indeed Life (itself), had they known!*"[4]

Worship is a means to remind us of this truth and instill it in our being. Warnings and contemplation remain in the realm of thought. The Quran tells us of the hereafter and all that we will face in that world and the narrations provide us with details of that life. All this is conceptual and may not provide us materialistic human beings enough to interact with. This is where these worships play an important role. They manifest the events of the hereafter in this life so we can feel them. Each act of worship is a microcosm of the hereafter and the path that we will take before we reach our eternal abode.

When we fast, we see in the thirst and hunger of the daytime in this world the prolonged thirst and hunger of the world of Resurrection, referred to as the Day of Judgment. We will stand in that world and await judgment at many sta-

---

[3] Al-Sadouq, *'Ilal Al-Sharae'*, 1:270. See also: Al-Majlisi, *Bihar Al-Anwar*, 93:370.
[4] The Holy Quran. Chapter 29 [The Spider; Arabic: *Al-'Ankabout*]. Verse 64.

tions for a long period of time. *"The angels and the Spirit ascend to Him in a day whose span is fifty thousand years."*[5]

Yet we live in heedlessness of that day. We are heedless of its thirst and hunger. Imam Ali (a) reminds us of this in a narration where he says,

> *In the [world of] Resurrection there shall be fifty stages, each lasting a thousand years. The first stage comes after resurrection from the grave, where they will be kept for a thousand years, naked, barefoot, hungry, and thirsty. Whoever is resurrected from his grave believing in his Lord, believing in his Lord's paradise and hell, believing in resurrection, reckoning and judgment, and admitting [belief for] God and believing in His Prophet (s), and all that has come from God the Exalted – he will be saved from the hunger and thirst...*[6]

We need to be reminded of this great horror. We don't only need a conceptual reminder but also a practical one. This is one manifestation of mercy that comes with this great worship. As the Prophet (s) says in his famous speech, *"and remember with your hunger and thirst [during the fast] the hunger of the Day of Resurrection and its thirst."*[7]

## Manifesting Servitude

One of the great levels that we should strive for is to manifest the true meaning of servitude in our selves. This is the principle purpose for our existence. The closer we are to

---

[5] The Holy Quran. Chapter 70 [Lofty Stations; Arabic: *al-Ma'arij*]. Verse 4.
[6] Al-Majlisi, *Bihar Al-Anwar*, 7:111.
[7] Al-Sadouq, *Al-Amali*, 154.

true servitude of God, the farther we become from servitude of other things such as wealth, power, and whimsical desires. We are either servants of God or servants of something else.

Each of us may claim that he is a servant of God. But what do we mean by that? Are we truly servants of God in the way that He has commanded us? Do we act according to His will in all aspects of our life? True servitude is a grand status and is achieved by only few of the most devout of his servants. Those servants never act according to their own wills and desires, but rather all their actions, speech, movement, and thoughts are in harmony with the will of God. This is not an easy task. It is truly the greatest struggle.

Servitude can be manifested in an individual through a number of characteristics. We will discuss a few of them below.

*Fearful Reverence*

**The Meaning of Fearful Reverence**. As we discussed in an earlier section, we use the word "reverence" in this book as a translation of the Arabic word "*Khushu*'." The English word reverence means "honor or respect felt or shown... profound adoring awed respect"[8] Every servant must have reverence for the Lord arising out of a deep awareness of God's presence. This awareness instills a sort of fear of God, not because God is out to get us but because God Almighty's presence is so overpowering. One with proper awareness would not want to fall out of God's favor. The more an individual comes to know of God and His majesty,

---

[8] Marriam Webster Dictionary.

His great power, and the greatness of His names and attributes, the more he grows fearful of Him, in a sense. That is why God says, *"Only those of God's servants having knowledge fear Him."*[9]

Fearful reverence is therefore not an easy attribute to attain. It depends on the individual's relationship with God. It depends on fear of God, which in turn depends on knowledge of Him. A person must work with dedication to achieve this high spiritual state.

**The Importance of Fearful Reverence.** This concept plays a great role in the life of mankind and our movement towards true servitude. God says,

> *Is it not time yet for those who have faith that their hearts should be [reverent] for God's remembrance and toward the truth which has come down [to them], and to be not like those who were given the Book before? Time took its toll on them and so their hearts were hardened, and many of them are transgressors.*[10]

God also says in praising Prophet Zacharias (a),

> *So We answered his prayer, and gave him John, and cured for him his wife [of infertility]. Indeed, they were active in [performing] good works, and they would supplicate Us with eagerness and awe and were [reverent] before Us.*[11]

Therefore, this reverence is a great characteristic that the prophets (a) possessed, and that we should all work tirelessly to attain.

---

[9] The Holy Quran. Chapter 35 [Arabic: *Fatir*]. Verse 28.
[10] The Holy Quran. Chapter 57 [The Iron; Arabic: *Al-Hadid*]. Verse 16.
[11] The Holy Quran. Chapter 21 [The Prophets; Arabic: *Al-Anbiya'*]. Verse 90.

**The Characteristics of the Reverent.** It is narrated that the Prophet (s) said, *"the traits of the reverent are four: observance of God['s commands] in private and in public, doing good, contemplating on the Day of Resurrection, and supplication to God."*[12] This is clearly indicative of knowledge of God and fear of Him. A reverent individual observes God's commands in private and in public so that he does not do anything that puts him farther from God. He does good for the sake of God. He thinks constantly of the hereafter, and fears to reach that world with what God displeases. He constantly supplicates to God because he knows and loves God.

*Humility*

At all times, God wants us to live not with weakness but with might, honor and decency. God says, *"They say, 'When we return to the city, the mighty will surely expel the weak from it.' Yet all might belongs to God and His Apostle and the faithful, but the hypocrites do not know."*[13]

This is true when it comes to human interactions. However, when we are speaking about an individual's relationship with God, the pinnacle of honor and decency comes in having humility towards God. Rather, humility is one of the signs of proximity and servitude to God.

There is no conflict between the two. When we have humility towards God and whoever God commands us to have humility towards, such as the prophets or our parents, we are attaining a higher level of servitude. Of course, God does not need our humility – He is the Independent and

---

[12] Al-Harrani, *Tuhaf Al-'Oqool*, 20.
[13] The Holy Quran. Chapter 63 [The Hypocrites; Arabic: *Al-Munafiqoon*]. Verse 8.

All-Sufficient. Humility rather brings benefits to the believer, as it brings him closer to true servitude.

*Servility*

Servility is a characteristic of weakness, submission, and humility before God. It is also of the characteristics that Islam promotes. And we see this concept repeated in many of the supplications taught to us by our Immaculate Imams (a).

## FASTING AS A MEANS TO REALIZING THESE TRAITS

The scholars of ethics focus much on hunger and the role that it plays in strengthening the self against desires. They rely in this on a number of narrations, such as the following narration,

> *[During the Ascension, God said to the Prophet (s)] 'Oh Ahmad, if only you were to taste the sweetness of hunger, silence, solitude, and all that they impart.' The Prophet (s) said, 'Oh Lord, and what does hunger impart?' God said, 'wisdom, protection of the heart, proximity to me, constant sorrow, lightness of [one's] burden amongst people, and speaking the truth, and being careless as to whether he lives with ease or hardship.*[14]

The scholars of ethics have listed a number of benefits for hunger, including:

1. Purity of the heart. Hunger purifies and softens the heart, and prepares it for contemplation and

---

[14] Al-Majlisi, *Bihar Al-Anwar*, 74:22. Citing: Al-Daylami, *Irshad Al-Qulub*, Chapter 54.

knowledge of God. When a person fills his stomach, he may be weighed down by the food. This purity of the heart allows the individual to use contemplation to reach a greater degree of fear of God, ultimately leading him to reverence, humility, and servility. It is narrated that the Prophet (s) said, "*do not be satiated for then the light of knowledge is extinguished in your hearts.*"[15]

2. Humility: A person feels weakness and need when he is hungry. With this, heedlessness and ungratefulness for God's blessings begin to fade. The person then begins to gain humility and servility for God.
3. Softheartedness. A person holds a much softer heart when he is hungry. The softer a person's heart, the more he is pleased with worship.
4. Closeness to the truth: It is narrated that Imam Baqir (a) said, "*The farthest of creations from God are those with full stomachs.*"[16] It is also narrated that Imam Sadiq (a) said, "*The closest a servant is to God is when his stomach is light.*"[17]

## Attaining Moral Perfections

Knowledge alone does not fulfill an individual's true potential. What fulfills this potential for mankind are the ethical aspects of our lives. The Prophet (s) says, "*I have not been sent*

---

[15] Al-Majlisi, *Bihar Al-Anwar*, 67:71.
[16] Ibid, 63:331.
[17] Ibid.

*but to complete the best of morals.*"¹⁸ God praises the Prophet (s) for his morals – "*and indeed you possess a great character*"¹⁹. It is one of the greatest missions of the prophets to model and teach morals. God says, "*It is He who sent to the [people of Mecca] an apostle from among themselves, to recite to them His signs, to purify them, and to teach them the Book and wisdom, and earlier they had indeed been in manifest error.*"²⁰

It is such morals that elevate humanity above all other creatures. Without them, we degenerate to a level lower than beasts – "*Have you seen him who has taken his desire to be his god? Is it your duty to watch over him? Do you suppose that most of them listen or exercise their reason? They are just like cattle; indeed, they are further astray from the way.*"²¹

*The Role of Worship in Attaining Ethical Perfections*

Worship builds on and strengthens a number of moral characteristics through two main aspects.

Firstly, worships strengthen a person's ethics through the process of commitment. Simply committing to an act of worship has its significance. When a person commits to a practice of worship, he has submitted his will to God and acted in accordance to His will. This submission plays a large role in the purification of the self in addition to strengthening the will of the individual.

Secondly, the content of these worships have a direct effect on the individual's morality. Prayers play their role – "*Recite*

---

[18] Al-Huwayzi, *Nour Al-Thaqalayn*, 5:392.
[19] The Holy Quran. Chapter 68 [The Pen; Arabic: *Al-Qalam*]. Verse 4.
[20] The Holy Quran. Chapter 62 [Friday; Arabic: *Al-Jumu'a*]. Verse 2.
[21] The Holy Quran. Chapter 25 [The Criterion; Arabic: *Al-Furqan*]. Verses 43, 44.

what has been revealed to you of the Book, and maintain the prayer. Indeed the prayer restrains from indecent and wrongful conduct, and the remembrance of God is surely greater. And God knows whatever [deeds] you do."[22]

Fasting also has its role. God says, "*O you who have faith! Prescribed for you is fasting as it was prescribed for those who were before you, so that you may be God-wary.*"[23]

We find in the sermon of Lady Zahra (a) – that great sermon that she delivered in the mosque of the Prophet (s) after his death, where she laments the oppression that took place against her and against the Commander of the Faithful – a reference to different types of worships, along with all the specific effects that each one has. She said,

> *God has obligated faith as purification for you from polytheism, prayers as a cleansing for you from pride, fasting as an expression of dedication, the pilgrimage as an elevation of faith, justice as harmony for the hearts, obedience to us for regulation of the religion, and our divine leadership as a safeguard from division… prohibition from drinking wine as a transcendence above impurity, avoidance of defamation as a shield from damnation, resignation of theft as an affirmation of fidelity. God has forbidden ascribing of partners to Him for devotion to His lordship. So have wariness of God as he is worthy of it. And do not die except while you are Muslims.*[24]

---

[22] The Holy Quran. Chapter 29 [The Spider; Arabic: *Al-'Ankabout*]. Verse 45.
[23] The Holy Quran. Chapter 2 [The Cow; Arabic: *Al-Baqara*]. Verse 183.
[24] Al-Miyanji, *Mawaqif Al-Shia*, 1:460. Citing: Al-Tabrasi, *Al-Ihtijaj*, 1:134-146.

## Fasting and Ethical Excellence

Fasting has its own effects in pushing man towards ethical perfection. Briefly, the most important of its ethical aspects are as follows:

**Contravention of Desires.** God has imparted us with faculties and desires that we can use for the betterment of the human race. However, in our heedlessness, we may have abused these faculties and desires and used them for corruption and deviance. God says,

> The love of [worldly] allures, including women and children, accumulated piles of gold and silver, horses of mark, livestock, and farms has been made to seem decorous to mankind. Those are the wares of the life of this world, but the goodness of one's ultimate destination lies near God.[25]

Yet, we have fallen prey to our base desires and have become enslaved to them.

> Have you seen him who has taken his desire to be his god and whom God has led astray knowingly, set a seal upon his hearing and heart, and put a blindfold on his sight? So who will guide him after God [has consigned him to error]? Will you not then take admonition?[26]

God has made a number of worships, such as fasting, as a means to control these base desires. This allows us to be free from our debasing desires and to spend our lives instead seeking moral and spiritual elevation. Fasting strengthens the soul and supports it against the reign of these regressive desires.

---

[25] The Holy Quran. Chapter 3 [Arabic: *Aal Imran*]. Verse 14.
[26] The Holy Quran. Chapter 45 [Arabic: *Al-Jathia*]. Verse 23.

Some people may be overtaken with gluttony, such that they see no pleasure in life other than in food and proceed to sin for the sake of their bellies. The Holy Month of Ramadhan and the season of fasting come to remind us that we are not cattle whose only purpose is to eat and be fattened. It reminds us that we can take our share of lawful pleasures in this world, but we must transcend beyond debasing worldly pursuits so that we can improve the more important aspects of our lives.

Fasting does the same with sexual desires. The Prophet (s) is narrated to have said, *"O youth! Whoever among you is able to, let him get married. Whoever is not able, let him fast as it is a [means of maintaining chastity] for him."*[27]

Fasting also plays a role in strengthening the spirit and reminding the self of its weaknesses and deficiencies. This in turn strengthens all other moral characteristics.

**Empathy**. God has put us on this Earth and obliged us with a number of social duties. We are creatures that have both rights and obligations. We were not created frivolously. We therefore have responsibilities that we must fulfill. One of the most important of these responsibilities is to stand alongside each other in our journey through this world.

People are different in their wealth and social status; that is a reality of life.

> *Is it they who dispense the mercy of your Lord? It is We who have dispensed among them their livelihood in the present life, and raised some of them above others in rank, so*

---

[27] Al-Nouri, *Mustadrak Al-Wasael*, 7:507.

*that some may take others into service, and your Lord's mercy is better than what they amass.*[28]

When a person sees that a fellow human being is in need, he may decide to take one of a number of positions. Some may be indifferent to that need, a position that is obviously depraved. Others may feel that it is not their responsibility; God has referred to this group of people in the verse "*When they are told, 'Spend out of what God has provided you,' the faithless say to the faithful, 'Shall we feed [someone] whom God would feed, if He wished? You are only in manifest error.*"[29] This group is heedless of the fact that God is providing sustenance and blessings to all, and that God wanted to test him with the duty of caring for others.

The third position that can be taken is the ethically correct one; to feel responsibility towards others. This level of morality and conscience is what separates mankind from the beasts. This attribute comes through empathy for the needs of others. Empathy plays a large role in strengthening moral attributes. Empathy is a characteristic of righteous and rational individuals, and acting in a way befitting of that empathy is a form of generosity.

Our Immaculate Imams (a) have always stressed and emphasized our duty to empathize with and console others. It is narrated that Imam Sadiq (a) said, "*We do not command any wrongdoing, but we command you to observe piety, piety, piety and [empathy along with consoling], [empathy along with consoling], [empathy along with consoling] of your brothers. The righteous servants of*

---

[28] The Holy Quran. Chapter 43 [Arabic: *Al-Zukhruf*]. Verse 32.
[29] The Holy Quran. Chapter 36 [Arabic: *Yaseen*]. Verse 47.

*God have always been abased and few in numbers since God created Adam (a)."*[30]

This is in addition to the significance of empathy along with consoling others as an indication of thinking well of God. A reasonable and cognizant person will know that God is the one that sustains everyone and that this is only a test for him. He will know that what he spends for the sake of God will not be lost and that he will be rewarded for it. The ignorant and heedless will think badly of God and believe that spending his wealth in this way will lead him to poverty. Fasting acts as a reminder of the needs of others and our duty to empathize with and console others. As Imam Rida (a) said, fasting was made an obligation for mankind *"so that they come to know the severity of what strikes the poor and destitute in this world, so they give them what God has obligated [as alms] from their wealth...."*[31]

Fasting acts as a reminder for those who are heedless of this truth. The hunger of fasting reminds us of the hunger of the poor. It reminds us of our duty to care for those less fortunate; a duty that God is testing us with as He is bestowing on us all of His countless blessings.

---

[30] Al-Barqi, *Al-Mahasin*, 1:158.
[31] Al-Sadouq, *'Ilal Al-Sharae'*, 1:270. See also: Al-Majlisi, *Bihar Al-Anwar*, 93:370.

# CHARITY

*In the Name of God the Beneficent the Merciful*

*The parable of those who spend their wealth in the way of God is that of a grain which grows seven ears, in every ear a hundred grains. God enhances several-fold whomever He wishes, and God is all-bounteous, all-knowing. Those who spend their wealth in the way of God and then do not follow up what they have spent with reproaches and affronts, they shall have their reward near their Lord, and they will have no fear, nor will they grieve. An honorable reply [in response to the needy] and forgiving [their annoyance] is better than a charity followed by affront. God is all-sufficient, most forbearing. O you who have faith! Do not render your charities void by reproaches and affronts, like those who spend their wealth to be seen by people and have no faith in God and the Last Day. Their parable is that of a rock covered with soil: a downpour strikes it, leaving it bare. They have no power over anything of what they have earned, and God does not guide the faithless lot. The parable of those who spend their wealth seeking God's pleasure and to confirm themselves [in their faith], is that of a garden on a hillside:*

*the downpour strikes it, whereupon it brings forth its fruit twofold; and if it is not a downpour that strikes it, then a shower, and God watches what you do.*[1]

These verses speak of a topic that is of utmost importance for the advancement of the community and in building human civilization. The topic of charity is one of the topics that is greatly emphasized in Islam, as it plays an essential role in creating a community that is built on sound values and principles, and that averts the pitfalls that other communities may plunge into.

Islam views the right religion as the one that addresses all matters of human life and provides the guidance for justice in all respects, guaranteeing happiness in this world and the next. Perhaps one of the most important means by which Islam regulates the community and solves its problems is through charity. Charity is regarded by God as an act of piety – those *"who believe in the Unseen, maintain the prayer, and spend out of what We have provided for them [in charity]."*[2]

## Economic Inequality

Islam holds that there is wisdom in economic inequality in human society, as it plays a significant role in the advancement of humanity and the building of civilization. The Holy Quran points to this truth in the verse

*Is it they who dispense the mercy of your Lord? It is We who have dispensed among them their livelihood in the present life, and raised some of them above others in rank, so*

---

[1] The Holy Quran. Chapter 2 [The Cow; Arabic: *Al-Baqara*]. Verses 261-65.
[2] The Holy Quran. Chapter 2 [The Cow; Arabic: *Al-Baqara*]. Verse 3.

*that some may take others into service, and your Lord's mercy is better than what they amass.*³

Economic inequality serves the interests of humanity as a whole. Without it, we would not have been able to build civilization or create marvelous constructions on this Earth. For if mankind were equal in economic capabilities, no one would provide any service to the other. Rather it is this inequality that creates interdependence between people and creates the basis for a functioning economic structure. Of course, Islam still comes with the rules necessary to regulate this relationship and ensure that the rights of each individual are secured, as we will see in this chapter.

However, there is a big difference between Islam's belief in Economic inequality and the belief in a class or caste system. Islam does not believe in class structure in society; meaning that wealth does not create preference for some individuals over others. Rather, the only thing that creates preference among individuals in society is their piety – "*Indeed the noblest of you in the sight of God is the most God-wary among you.*"⁴ As the Prophet (s) said, "*Oh people! Your Lord is one, and your father is one. You are all of Adam (a) and Adam (a) is of dust. The noblest of you in the sight of God is the most pious. No Arab has any preference over a non-Arab, except if he were more pious….*"⁵

So Islam holds that there is wisdom behind economic inequality, but does not believe that social, political, or religious status should be based on wealth.

---

³ The Holy Quran. Chapter 43 [Arabic: *Al-Zukhruf*]. Verse 32.
⁴ The Holy Quran. Chapter 49 [Arabic: *Al-Hojorat*]. Verse 13.
⁵ Al-Majlisi, *Bihar Al-Anwar*, 73:350.

## ISLAM AND THE WEALTHY

Islam does not have a negative outlook towards the wealthy in and of themselves. To the contrary, Islam encourages trade and seeking a livelihood. Indeed, Islam was built on the wealth of Lady Khadija (a), who was herself a merchant. Islam believes that if these people act according to the teachings of Islam, they become a great asset to the community. With their wealth, they can build social and educational institutions and contribute greatly to building the community as a whole. It's erroneous to think that Islam takes a negative stance from the wealthy. Abu Basir (r), a companion of Imam Baqir (a), narrates the following,

> *We mentioned in the presence of [Imam Baqir] (a) a number of the wealthy amongst the Shia, and he seemed displeased with what we said. He said,* 'Oh Abu [Basir], if a believer was wealthy as well as merciful, pleasant, and kind to his companions, God will give him the rewards of what he spends in righteousness a doubled reward. God the Exalted says "It is not your wealth, nor your children, that will bring you close to Us in nearness, excepting those who have faith and act righteously. It is they for whom there will be a twofold reward for what they did."[6][7]

Therefore, the wealthy are a pillar of the community that everyone else relies upon; conditioned, of course, on the premise that they abide by Islamic teachings and care for the needs of the community.

---

[6] The Holy Quran. Chapter 34 [Arabic: *Saba*]. Verse 37.
[7] Al-Sadouq, *'Ilal Al-Sharae'*, 2:604.

The blessing of wealth is a test for this group of individuals. They are being tested on whether they will be grateful or ungrateful. It's not only a verbal expression of gratefulness that is expected, but a practical one that comes through charitable spending. A scholar who is blessed with knowledge must practice practical gratefulness through spreading the knowledge that he has earned. A scholar who is blessed with the skill that is required to cure the ill must practice practical gratefulness through providing medical care and fighting illnesses and anyone who is blessed with any sort of wealth must practice practical gratitude by spending for the sake of God. It is narrated that Imam Rida (a) said,

> *Know that you will never be grateful to God with anything – after [showing gratitude by having] faith in God and His Prophet (s), and admission of the rights of the vicegerents from the Household of Muhammad (a) – that is more beloved to you than [showing gratitude by] aiding your believing brothers in their lives of this world that are their bridge to the paradises of their Lord.*[8]

No one should think that charitable spending is an obligation on one group of people and not on others. It's not an obligation of the powerful as opposed to the weak. It is not an obligation on the wealthy as opposed to the middle class. Some people may have a higher responsibility than others, but everyone shares the obligation. As the Prophet (s) used to say, *"Safeguard yourself from hellfire even if it were by [giving] a piece of a date."*[9]

---

[8] Al-Majlisi, *Bihar Al-Anwar*, 75:355.
[9] Al-Sadouq, *Al-Amali*, 154.

## Preserving the Muslim Community

Islam regards the Muslim community as a single body; the Prophet (s) said, *"The example of the believers in their affection, mercy, and compassion for each other is that of a single body. When any limb aches, the whole body reacts with sleeplessness and fever."*[10] Each member of this body has rights over all others and has obligations towards them. That is why Islam took painstaking efforts in regulating wealth so as to protect the unity of the community and to create an equitable society. Islam forbids squandering of wealth, encouraging people to spend their money wisely and appropriately. One of the benefits of Islam's emphasis on charity is to elevate the poor's standard of living. This can help prevent wealth from creating enmity and division within society, leading to disorder and war. This is one way how charitable spending is a factor of stability within the Muslim community.

The Muslim community during the time of the Prophet (s) gives us a prime example of how charity, no matter how little, can lead to a happy and harmonious community. During the time of the Prophet (s), the Muslims would sacrifice for one another and split their wealth amongst themselves. Despite the very small financial capabilities that they had, they provided us a great example of magnanimity and use of wealth to advance the individuals making up the community.

What good is living in a large home or driving a luxurious car if the person does not possess the spirit of humanity within him? What good is grandiose architecture if it is

---

[10] Al-Hindi, *Kanz Al-'Ummal*, 1:149.

empty of all affection and brotherhood? The rich should look to the poor as a brother who needs help. Instead, some of us may be consumed with greed and choose to exploit others. Regardless, there are still some – albeit dim – glimmers of the spirit of Islam still living with us. We see some charitable works that attempt to take care of the poor. But they do not measure up to what Islam aspires to.

One of the greatest crimes a person can commit is to hoard his wealth while others are in need.

> *Those who treasure up gold and silver, and do not spend it in the way of God, inform them of a painful punishment on the day when these shall be heated in hellfire and therewith branded on their foreheads, their sides, and their backs [and told]: 'This is what you treasured up for yourselves! So taste what you have treasured!'*[11]

When some are hoarding their wealth and freezing it in a bank account while others are hungry and destitute, God regards it as a crime against Him. Especially when the rich do not fulfill their obligatory alms; that is a great crime of ungratefulness to God. Indeed, Imam Ali (a) points to this phenomenon with admonition,

> *You are in a period when [signs of] virtue are receding, [signs of] of evil are proceeding, and Satan is increasing his eagerness to ruin people. This is the time that his equipment is strong, his traps have been spread, and his prey has become easy [to catch]. [Look at people all around!] Do you see anything but a poor man suffering from poverty? Or a*

---

[11] The Holy Quran. Chapter 9 [The Repentance; Arabic: *Al-Tawba*]. Verses 34, 35.

*rich man ungrateful to God despite His bounty? Or a miser increasing his wealth by trampling on God's obligations? Or a mischievous person closing his ears to all counsel?*[12]

## THE QUALITY OF CHARITABLE GIVING

So is there a specific way and method for charitable giving? Or is charity of all types the same? Is there anything beyond the economics of inequality that Islam looks at?

We see that many nations impose taxes as a sort of compulsory charity. In such systems, the spiritual aspect of giving is usually disregarded. The only aim of such systems is to reallocate wealth so as to care for the poor and provide essential services.

The type of charitable giving that Islam espouses has a spiritual dimension as well. A person must give seeking closeness to God. Indeed, this is a condition in some forms of obligatory charity in Islam. The spiritual dimension of giving has an impact on one's relationship with God Almighty. Moreover, when it comes to the obligatory alms – whether it be *khums, zakat,* or any other monetary obligation – Islam places the responsibility of fully fulfilling the obligation upon the individual. One might mischievously be able to fool worldly authorities, but no one can fool God Almighty. Furthermore, while the obligatory forms of charity are limited, one is also encouraged to give of what one holds most dear on a voluntary basis – *"You will never attain piety until you spend out of what you hold dear."*[13]

---

[12] Al-Radi, *Nahj Al-Balagha,* Sermon 129.
[13] The Holy Quran. Chapter 3 [Arabic: *Aal Imran*]. Verse 92.

# The Quantity of Charitable Giving

Islam thus focuses on the quality of charitable giving and not simply its quantity. A person may give millions but for ulterior motives, and Islam does not regard this act as praiseworthy if the intention is malign. On the other hand, a person could give a very simple gift for the sake of God, and that gift will have great value. *"Those who give their wealth by night and day, secretly and openly, they shall have their reward near their Lord, and they will have no fear, nor will they grieve."*[14] Our scholars tell us that this verse was revealed in praise of Imam Ali (a), after he had given away all the money that he had – four dinars at the time – part at night and part during the day, part in secret and part in public.[15] Even though the four dinars hold very little value, the pure intention that accompanied the giving elevated the value of the act so that it was so praiseworthy in the eyes of God.

We need to learn two very important lessons from this story. First, we need to give out of our own free will and with full dedication and devotion to God. Otherwise, our act of giving is not worth much. Second, we cannot take the hardships that we might go through as an excuse not to give in the way of God. One meal given for the sake of God could be greater than millions. We should not deny ourselves the blessings of this great act simply because we do not think that we can afford to give anything. Something that is seen to be little materialistically may not be small spiritually and sentimentally.

---

[14] The Holy Quran. Chapter 2 [The Cow; Arabic: *Al-Baqara*]. Verse 274.
[15] Al-Tabatabaei, *Al-Mizan*, 2:406.

# Forms of Charitable Giving

The Holy Quran mentioned a number of forms in which charitable giving may come, some of which are correct while others are incorrect. God provided examples of each so we can more easily understand the consequences that they carry.

## Giving for the Sake of God

The acceptable form of giving in the eyes of the divine legislator is that which is undertaken with the intention of seeking closeness to God. Because of its righteous nature, it bears great positive consequences. God says,

> *The parable of those who spend their wealth seeking God's pleasure and to confirm themselves [in their faith], is that of a garden on a hillside: the downpour strikes it, whereupon it brings forth its fruit twofold; and if it is not a downpour that strikes it, then a shower, and God watches what you do.*[16]

So long as a person starts with the right intention – that of pleasing God – when he gives his charitable contribution to society and maintains that right intention, what he has given will grow and be multiplied manifold for him in the hereafter. God compares this type of giving to a fertile land; whether it receives heavy or light rain, it will bear fruits, but its fruits will be multiplied with heavy rains. By this example, God is telling us that he will reward us for our generous giving, but that the level of reward will be different depending on the purity of our intention and level of sincerity.

---

[16] The Holy Quran. Chapter 2 [The Cow; Arabic: *Al-Baqara*]. Verse 265.

When the act is built on a strong conviction and love for God with intense sincerity, it will be like a downpour and it will multiply the fruits of the action. But when the act is built on a sincere albeit less intensely sincere intention, it will be like a shower and we will receive a lesser reward.

## Duplicity in Charitable Giving

The Quran gives us another example of the forms of giving; giving that is not based on a pure intention in seeking closeness to God, but on duplicity, pride, and vainglory.

> *O you who have faith! Do not render your charities void by reproaches and affronts, like those who spend their wealth to be seen by people and have no faith in God and the Last Day. Their parable is that of a rock covered with soil: a downpour strikes it, leaving it bare. They have no power over anything of what they have earned, and God does not guide the faithless lot.*[17]

This form of giving will not bear fruits, and will not be rewarding to the giver in the Hereafter. Although soil and rain are essential to the cultivation of plants, the soil is simply washed away if the surface upon which the soil rests is hard. Hence, nothing will grow there. The problem is neither with the soil nor with the rain. The problem is in having the soil rely on a hard surface that easily allows the soil to be washed away. Similarly, while giving charity has the propensity to be rewarding, if it comes from a heart with the wrong intention, that heart cannot cultivate the true rewards of charity. Such a heart has sealed itself off from the Divine

---

[17] The Holy Quran. Chapter 2 [The Cow; Arabic: *Al-Baqara*]. Verse 264.

showers of mercy. The problem lies in the insincere heart upon which the charitable act relied.

Moreover, God ends the verse with the statement "and God does not guide the faithless lot."[18] This is an indication that those who practice duplicity while giving charity are lacking in faith as they perform that action. The faithless have chosen to turn away from guidance. God does not guide the faithless.

*Spending with Reproaches and Affronts*

It is possible that giving can be initiated with a great intention, but is later transformed by the giver into a vice. God says,

> *Would any of you like to have a garden of palm trees and vines, with streams running in it, with all kinds of fruit for him therein, and old age were to strike him while he has weakly offspring; whereupon a fiery hurricane were to hit it, whereat it lies burnt? Thus does God clarify His signs for you so that you may reflect.*[19]

Spending with pure intentions results in great consequences; manifested in this parable as gardens of trees, vines, streams, and fruits. However, it may be struck with a hurricane carrying a fire and all will be lost. Moreover, the person may be weak and unable to rebuild this beautiful garden. His children may be incapable of helping him as well. Those rewards that he had earned by his good will and actions can be burned away by his wretched choices and he may not be able to gain them back.

---

[18] The Holy Quran. Chapter 2 [The Cow; Arabic: *Al-Baqara*]. Verse 264.
[19] The Holy Quran. Chapter 2 [The Cow; Arabic: *Al-Baqara*]. Verse 266.

These are a few of the forms of charitable giving that are addressed in the Holy Quran.

# PILGRIMAGE

*In the Name of God the Beneficent the Merciful*

*When We settled for Abraham the site of the House [saying], Do not ascribe any partners to Me, and purify My House for those who circle around it, and those who stand [in it for prayer], and those who bow and prostrate themselves. And proclaim the Hajj to all the people: they will come to you on foot and on lean camels, coming from distant places, that they may witness the benefits for them, and mention God's Name during the known days over the livestock He has provided them. So eat thereof and feed the destitute and the needy.*[1]

One of the greatest acts of worship is that which God tested His servants with in order to see the sincerity of their servitude and subservience. He ordered them to direct themselves to a barren land of sanctuaries to fulfill their obligation of servitude and obedience as a test from God. This season of pilgrimage is a season of honor and purification for the believer. The believer immerses himself in the worship of God, letting go of material things and covering him-

---

[1] The Holy Quran. Chapter 22 [The Pilgramige; Arabic: Al-Hajj]. Verses 26-28.

self with the simplest of cloth. In this movement of worship, he gains a readiness to destroy his inner idols of whim and ignorance. He also gains a propensity to direct himself completely in worship of his one and only god– God (swt).

The season of Hajj has many lessons to offer, both to those who embark on the journey and those who stay behind. The most important of these lessons are reflected in learning the benefits that a believer enjoys from this unique act of worship.

## The Material Benefits of Hajj

There is no doubt that upon reading the Quranic verse above, one of benefits that comes to mind is the benefit that is gained in this world via buying, selling, and earning that comes from this season. Are the benefits of this unique worship reserved in buying and selling? Or do the benefits of the pilgrimage encompass something much greater? The above verse is not limited to the financial benefits that come with this season, because in reality only a small group of people actually benefit monetarily from Hajj. Many people on the other hand may believe they are on the losing end monetarily, as they give their money to embark on the journey or support others to do so. Thus, it only makes sense that the greater benefit of the pilgrimage would include much more than monetary transactional gain. The benefits can be categorized into three groups:

*Trade & Commerce*

With the spirituality that comes with the season of Hajj, the time is also considered to be a season of trade and commerce. When we review the narrations of Ahlulbayt (a) we notice that they acknowledged the monetary benefits that came with the season. Hisham bin Al-Hakam, one of the companions of Imam Al-Sadiq (a), asked the Imam (a), "Why did God make the Pilgrimage an obligation upon His servants?" The Imam (a) mentioned a number of the benefits of the pilgrimage in a lengthy conversation, which included:

> *And [so that] every people would take away some trades from country to country, and the [guides] and the cameleers would benefit… If each community were to [suffice itself with] its own lands and what is in it, they would perish, the lands would be ruined, and [imports] and profits would subside…*[2]

The Hajj brings wealth and repels poverty from the pilgrims. The Commander of the Faithful (a) said in one of his sermons, *"the Hajj and the Umrah to the House of God, for they repel poverty and wash away sin."*[3] It may seem strange that these great rituals, along with the paying of the alms, are worships that require personal expenditure, and yet God promises wealth to whoever makes such expenditures. But with God, the equation is not merely materialistic.

## *Assembly of the Believers*

The assembly of the believers from the different corners of the world, despite their diversity in ethnicity, race, language, and culture, can strengthen the spiritual and religious bond between them. The interchange of cultures and ideas can

---

[2] Al-Amili, *Wasael Al-Shia*, 8:9.
[3] Al-Radi, *Nahj Al-Balagha*, 1:215.

result in greater and deeper benefits for all sides. This also has a propensity to ferment a feeling of strength in faith; as each pilgrim sees the waves of believers of all backgrounds encircling the House of God in worship of Him. He may begin to feel that the strength of the millions of believers working towards the goal of reaching God, the Exalted. He will see the millions that believe in the Quran as the word of God and take the Holy Prophet (s) as an example in their lives. This can bring about a sense of pride and strengthen the believer's faith. This allows him to stand against his own base desires, as well as the corruptions and deviances of the world.

*Breaking the Routine of Everyday Life*

There is no doubt that a person who lives a tedious and monotonous life may face many emotional and psychological problems, which in turn reflect on the community and create a lot of social problems therein. This is why we see some doctors advise their patients to change the pace of their lives by taking a vacation and a break from one's daily routine. But in many vacations and travels, people are not able to break their daily routine entirely. However, in the Hajj, the believer changes his entire life – food, drink, clothing, habitation, and all other aspects. This is in addition to the great spiritual significance of the pilgrimage that takes him away from the worries of everyday life. After that trip, a believer is likely to return to his homeland inspired and reinvigorated. This may be the indication of the narration attributed to Imam Sadiq (a). Imam Sadiq (a) says, "[*Imam*] *Ali* son of Hussein (a) said: perform the Hajj and the Umrah,[4] your bodies will become healthy and your sustenance will grow..."[5] Moreover, there is no doubt that the peace that this experience can bring has a great impact on the individual's life.

It may seem strange that one performing this ritual is promised better health since we see many of those who return from the Hajj coming back sick due to all the viruses that are carried from around the world. However, many narrations tell us that the Hajj provides better health for the pilgrim. Maybe it is exactly these viruses that bring better health, as being exposed to these viruses may strengthen the individual's immunity. Or there may be another explanation for this that we do not yet understand. Nevertheless, this is indicated by the narrations of the Holy Household (a) including the narration we mentioned above – "*[Imam] Ali son of Hussein (a) said: perform the Hajj and the Umrah, your bodies will become healthy and your sustenance will grow...*"

## THE SPIRITUAL BENEFITS OF HAJJ

One of the companions of Imam Sadiq (a) narrates the following:

> *I saw [Imam Sadiq (a)] while he was circling the Kaaba carried on a sedan chair while he was gravely ill. Every time*

---

[4] Umrah is a set of rituals performed by Muslims out of devotion to God. Like Hajj, Umrah may be obligatory in certain cases and may be recommended in others. Also like Hajj, it is of two types, *ifrad* and *tamattu'*. For details, see *Manasik al-Hajj*, by Grand Ayatollah Sayyid Sistani.

[5] Al-Kulayni, *Al-Kafi*, 4:252.

*he would reach Al-Rukn Al-Yamani,*[6] *he would ask that he is put down. He would stretch his hand out and drag it on the floor. He would then [ask to be raised and the rituals continued]. When I saw that he did this persistently in every time around, I said to him, 'may I be sacrificed for your sake, Oh son of the Messenger of God! This is hard on you [in your current condition].' He said, 'I heard God the Exalted say, "that they may witness the benefits for them."*[7] *I asked him whether [the verse refers to] the benefit of the material world or the benefits of the hereafter. He replied, 'both.'*[8]

## Worship

In Hajj, the pilgrim performs a number of rituals out of devotion to God and seeks the benefits and rewards of all of these rituals – prayer, fasting, alms, charity, and others. In this sense, Hajj is a microcosm of all worships.

## Spirituality

There is no doubt that the Hajj deepens the individual's connection with the unseen. This is especially due to the unordinary nature of the rituals of the Hajj. It is narrated that the Commander of the Faithful (a) described this in one of his sermons, saying:

*Do you not see that God, the Glorified, has tried all people – from the very beginning with Adam, to the last of mankind – with stones that yield neither benefit nor harm, and*

---

[6] The southern corner of the Kaaba. This corner of the Kaaba has great significance. It is narrated that the Prophet (s) used to touch this corner frequently. See: Al-Reyshahri, *Al-Haj wa al-'Umrah fi al-Kitab wa al-Sunnah*, 112.

[7] The Holy Quran. Chapter 22 [The Pilgramige; Arabic: Al-Hajj]. Verse 28.

[8] Al-Kulayni, *Al-Kafi*, 4:422.

> *that neither see nor hear. He made those stones into His Sacred House which He made a place of worship for the people. He placed it in the most rugged stony part of the earth and on a highland with the least soil thereon. He placed it among the narrowest valleys between rough mountains, soft sandy plains, springs of scanty water, and scattered villages. [A land] where neither camels nor horses nor cows and sheep could prosper.*

The Imam (a) first describes the holy lands and the hardship of their terrain, the shortage of their waters, and the heat of their climates. Then he would say,

> *Then He commanded Adam and his sons to turn their [attention] towards it. In this way it became the center of their journeys... so that human spirits hasten toward it from distant waterless deserts, deep and low lying valleys, and scattered islands in the seas. They shake their shoulders in humbleness and recite the slogan of having reached His [Holy Land]. They march with swift feet, disheveled hair, and dusted faces. They throw their pieces of cloth behind their backs. They have marred the beauty of their faces by leaving their hair uncut. [It is surely] a great test, a severe tribulation, an open trial, and an extreme examination....*

The Imam (a) then further explains the wisdom behind all this.

> *If God, the Glorified, had placed His sacred House and His great signs among plantations, streams, soft and level plains, plenty of trees, an abundance of fruits, a dense population, close villages, golden wheat, lush gardens, green land, plentiful parcels, thriving orchards and crowded streets, the amount of recompense would have decreased because of the*

> *ease of the trial… But God tries His creatures by means of different troubles, wants them to render worship through hardships, and involves them in distresses, all in order to extract the vanity within their hearts and to humble their souls. He makes all this an open door for His favors and an easy means for His forgiveness.*[9]

All these rites and rituals that we may perform without knowing the specific wisdom behind them; they are means of worship and a test for us. This worship of God sprouts from belief in and connection to the unseen. It allows for the height of spirituality.

## Forgiveness

There is no doubt that the Hajj is one of the most important worships for those seeking forgiveness. The Commander of the Faithful (a) said in one of his sermons, "*the Hajj and the Umrah to the House of God, for they repel poverty and wash away sin.*"[10]

A person who approaches God the Exalted with full sincerity to worship Him as He desires, he will surely be forgiven.

This is in addition to the fact that the Hajj is a process for protection against sin and deviance. It provides the individual with the necessary strength of spirit and sense of reverence for God that softens the heart. All this and other factors drive the individual away from sin and deviance.

---

[9] Al-Radi, *Nahj Al-Balagha*, 2:146.
[10] Ibid, 1:215.

# Enjoining Good

*In the Name of God the Beneficent the Merciful*

*Ask them about the town that was situated on the seaside, when they violated the Sabbath, when their fish would come to them on the Sabbath day, visibly on the shore, but on days when they were not keeping Sabbath they would not come to them. Thus did We test them because of the transgressions they used to commit. When a group of them said, 'Why do you advise a people whom God will destroy, or punish with a severe punishment?' They said, 'As an excuse before your Lord, and [with the hope] that they may be Godwary.' So when they forgot what they had been reminded of, We delivered those who forbade evil [conduct] and seized the wrongdoers with a terrible punishment because of the transgressions they used to commit.*[1]

## About the Honorable Verses

These noble verses shed light on a subject of the utmost importance, and that is the topic of 'enjoining the good and

---

[1] The Holy Quran. Chapter 7 [The Heights; Arabic: *Al-A'raf*]. Verses 163-165.

forbidding the evil.' God teaches us these principles in the Holy Quran by way of stories, "*We relate to you the best of parables...*"[2] Through these narratives that took place in history, having their effects on people and society, we are better able to understand the lessons and principles of God. We notice that the Holy Quran gives much focus in relating the stories of the Children of Israel, given that the message of Moses (a) was one that dealt with all aspects of life. His message was legislation for all the matters of life, very similar to the message of Muhammad (s) in this regard. Islam is a religion that addresses the human being from all aspects; his relationship with God, his conduct and behavior, and his relationship with society. Thus, perhaps given the similarity in the two messages God gives us many examples from the time of Moses (a) so that we, as the followers of Muhammad (s), can relate and see the effects that come with observing God's law.

The verse above describes a group of the Children of Israel that lived near the shore of the sea. God wished to test and try them – which is a divine tradition in God's relationship with His servants. God forbade them from fishing on Saturday – the Sabbath. What made the test even more difficult was that this group noticed that, particularly on Saturday, the fish would be so great in number they would appear near the surface of the water making them very easy to catch. On the other days of the week, however, fish did not appear much and they were much more difficult to catch. The group couldn't resist their urge to catch the easy fish of the Sabbath so they disobeyed God's commands. They

---

[2] The Holy Quran. Chapter 12 [Joseph; Arabic: *Yusuf*]. Verse 3.

would set up their nets on Saturday and take them out the following day. Some of them would create traps to corner the fish, so that they could fish the following day with a huge number of fish in one isolated area. The community then split into three categories. The first group was comprised of the individuals that continued to fish on the Sabbath, neglecting the will of God and disobeying His commands. The second group did not fish but they would stand and watch as the first group did. They did not try to advise the first group to stop what they were doing. What was worse was that when others would want to come and advise the first group to stop fishing, this second group would attempt to deter them by saying that God is responsible for the punishment.

The third group was comprised of those individuals who did not engage in the fishing activities on the Sabbath and advised people against falling into that sin. They believed that if they could remind others and discourage them from sin that they would repent and come back to God. They believed despite the fact that the first group may not repent, at least they had done what was their responsibility and had a legitimate excuse before God in their relationship with the rest of society. The first group, however, continued to pursue the prohibited fishing on Saturday and did not heed to the third group's advice. Thus, God sent down his punishment upon those who transgressed. Sending down punishment as such was the divine tradition up until the time of the "Forgiven Nation" – the community of Muhammad (s). Punishment would come down on those who persisted in sin. This was lifted when God sent humanity the Mercy to the Worlds – Prophet Muhammad (s). No longer was such chastisement for the sinners made on Earth, for it became reserved only for the afterlife. When God sent his punishment to the Children of Israel in the story above, no one survived except the third group that refrained from the sin and advised the others to do the same. The first and second groups were considered oppressors by God and the punishment befell them both indiscriminately.

From this story you can see the significance of enjoining the good and forbidding the evil, as carried out by the third group. If we don't enjoin the good and forbid the evil we are likely to fall into the other groups that rejected the will of God.

Nonetheless, a question is posed: why was enjoining the good and forbidding the evil from among the most important obligations set by God?

This question can be answered in three primary points:

*Realizing the Goal of Creation*

The fundamental goal of creation is the absolute servitude to God alone. "*I did not create the jinn and the humans except that they may worship Me.*"[3] Each one of us intuitively realizes his/her responsibility to honor this mercy of God and with his/her free will, strive to achieve this great goal. We need to realize that any time we stray from this goal we are partnering with the oppressors in their oppression and the sinners in their sin in defying the will of God. It is narrated that Imam Al-Sadiq (a) said, "… *If he is to see evil and not reject it when he is able to, then he desires to for God to be defied. Whoever*

---

[3] The Holy Quran. Chapter 51 [Arabic: *Al-Dariyat*]. Verse 56.

*desires for God to be defied has challenged Him in enmity.*"[4] This is what the verse refers to. Whoever does not reject or change the evil that he sees, and does not care to change it, then he is considered to be a partner in that evil.

## *The Social Aspect*

Islam looks at society as one body, as narrated in the following noble tradition: "*The example of the believers in their love, mercy, and empathy is like that of a body; if one part of the body was pained, the rest of the body would fall into sleeplessness and fever.*"[5]

Even though we are judged individually for our conduct and behavior, and are not liable for the actions of others, we still have responsibilities towards the people around us. We have obligations to the society we live in. We can't expect to be on the path of God while ignoring what goes on in our communities. If corruption spreads within the communities we live in, we are naturally susceptible to being affected by such corruption because we live in that community. Think of the environment, pollution and disease. The healthier the environments and atmospheres we live in, the greater the chance that we will avoid getting infected with diseases. This applies in a similar way for spiritual diseases that are contracted through the environment and infused by social conduct, behavior and interaction.

Therefore, it makes sense that we would desire to be in better and purer environments to protect ourselves in our journey toward God. When we commit to enjoining the good and forbidding the evil we help create an atmosphere

---

[4] Al-Kulayni, *Al-Kafi*, 5:108.
[5] Al-Hindi, *Kanz Al-'Ummal*, 1:149.

of goodness and God-consciousness in our communities. Doing this will protect us from the spiritual diseases that, if untreated, only produces the detrimental outcome of God's displeasure and punishment.

*The Individual Aspect*

In addition to what we have mentioned of the necessity of building a good solid environment that helps us in our journey on the path of righteousness toward God, there is something else to keep in mind. This regard is for the individual, and can be discussed in two points:

**Strengthening Faith.** Enjoining the good and forbidding the evil aids a person in his commitment to God. Generally, the more committed a person is to enjoining others in good and forbidding others from evil, the more careful and conscious he is of his own conduct, the less likely he is to fall into the evil he sees others falling into. *"It is greatly outrageous to God that you should say what you do not do."*[6]

But even if a person is not religiously committed to performing the good that he enjoins or to abstaining from the evil that he forbids, doing so could be the launching point for him to become religious and to better himself in that aspect. Someone came up to the Holy Prophet (s) and said, "O' Messenger of God, should we not enjoin in the good unless we completely act on that good and not forbid the evil unless we completely abandon that evil ourselves?" The Holy Prophet (s) responded, *"No, rather you should enjoin the*

---

[6] The Holy Quran. Chapter 61 [Arabic: *Al-Saff*]. Verse 3.

*good even if you don't act on it completely, and forbid the evil even if you don't abandon it completely [in your actions]."*[7]

**Being Excused Before God**. If you are able to affect the actions of others in enjoining the good and forbidding the evil, that is great. However, if you are unable to then you have at least performed your obligation and are excused of further responsibility before God. Helping others change and become better is an honorable deed; still, some people will not heed good advice. Thus, even if we are unsuccessful in helping others change we have at least carried out our personal obligation to God.

## Effects of Enjoining Good and Forbidding Evil

The effects and blessings of enjoining the good and forbidding the evil can be summarized in the following narration of Imam Al-Baqir (a):

> *Enjoining the good and forbidding the evil is the path of the prophets, the course of the good-doers, and is a great duty. With it [the other] obligations are carried out, the schools of thought are protected, honest livings are made, oppression is deterred, the Earth is [populated], one gets one's rights back from the enemies, and matters are set straight.*[8]

In his words, Imam Al-Baqir (a) describes to us that enjoining the good and forbidding the evil is the path of the prophets. The prophets were not sent except to establish justice and truth, and the way to that establishment came by

---

[7] Al-Amili, *Wasael Al-Shia*, 11:420.
[8] Al-Kulayni, *Al-Kafi*, 5:56.

means of calling people to commit to good and to reject evil. The righteous in those communities followed them in such accord; thus, the Imam (a) shows us that fulfilling this obligation is the groundwork for having stability and happiness in the community to be enjoyed by each of its members. With such stability, the rest of obligations are also carried out – any of the responsibilities that God has ordained for His servants to fulfill towards Him or towards others. This is so because enjoining the good and forbidding the evil provide a system that encourages people to fulfill their responsibilities and not neglect each other, themselves, or God. If someone strays from the path of guidance, there is a community there to help him get back on track and return to the path of his journey toward God.

The Imam (a) mentions another blessing that comes with enjoining the good and forbidding the evil – an honest living. A society that enjoins the good and forbids the evil ensures that its members collectively only seek livelihood by honest means. The members of society will only advise one another in ways that are honest and fair instead of encouraging one another to cheat, gamble, and steal. If done properly, such a community will shield itself from all harm because it has a defense mechanism that repels wrongdoing and nurtures righteousness.

In addition, Imam Al-Baqir (a) points to deterring oppression through enjoining the good and forbidding the evil. The oppressed is saved from the oppressor and the oppressor is deterred from oppressing. It is only natural that if people were to actually enjoin one another in good and dissuade one another from wrongdoing, that God's blessings would shower upon them because of their strong dedication and immersion in His remembrance.

If you, your family, and your livelihood are secured on all levels, what better state of happiness could you ask for? You are far from any spiritual or physical diseases that come by way of eating what is prohibited. You are in harmony with your environment and the world around you. All of this is possible through the blessings of enjoining the good and forbidding the evil.

Some may think that enjoining the good and forbidding the evil will instead have a person fall into problems and hardship. A person would be mistaken to adopt such thinking. Our narrations from Ahlulbayt (a) completely negate this mentality. Imam Ali (a) said, *"Enjoining good and forbidding evil do not hasten death, nor do they decrease sustenance. And better than all of that is [to speak] a word of justice before an oppressive governor."*[9] Both history and divine tradition are witnesses to this reality. One's death will not come any nearer if God has written for each person a certain time that no one can change but He. One's sustenance will not be decreased if God ordains the livelihood for each person that cannot be limited by any other. This promise that the Imam (a) gives is a reassurance of our responsibility and commitment to fulfilling this path, which is the path of the prophets and the course of the righteous. The God who guarantees our existence and our sustenance is the God who commands us to enjoin the good and forbid the evil.

---

[9] Al-Radi, *Nahj Al-Balagha*, 4:90, Short Saying 374.

## Negative Effects of Neglecting this Duty

To neglect fulfilling this obligation is to bring upon one's self negative consequences and effects. Evil befalls such a person, his prayers are not answered, God's punishment sets upon him, and his blessings will be stripped away from him. This is only natural, because to neglect this obligation and be content with seeing others do wrong and injustice is a grave sin. Just as God punished the Children of Israel for not forbidding the evil of those who did not observe the Sabbath, we are not exempt from the consequences of angering God due to abandoning our own responsibility.

The Commander of the Faithful (a) advised, *"Do not neglect enjoining the good and forbidding the evil, for then the most evil amongst you will [be put in charge of you]. Then you will supplicate [to God] and you will not be answered."*[10]

The Holy Prophet (s) said, *"Surely you are to enjoin the good and forbid the evil, or [else,] indeed the punishment of God will encompass you."*[11]

It is also narrated that the Holy Prophet (s) said,

> My nation will remain in a good state so long as they enjoin the good, forbid the evil, and collaborate for righteousness. If they do not, then the blessings will be stripped away from them, they will turn against one another, and they will have no one to support them in the heavens or on Earth.[12]

---

[10] Ibid, 3:77.
[11] Al-Amili, *Wasael Al-Shia*, 11:407.
[12] Ibid, 11:398.

# Modesty

*In the Name of God the Beneficent the Merciful*

*O Prophet! Tell your wives and your daughters and the women of the faithful to draw closely over themselves their chadors [when going out]. That makes it likely for them to be recognized and not be troubled, and God is all-forgiving, all-merciful.*[1]

## Reality versus Impressions

Not only do women comprise half of society, more or less – without women the other half of society would not exist. Women have significant roles that men simply cannot fulfill, let alone the roles that women can fulfill just as well as or even better than men. Prior to the advent of Islam, women were not held in the honorable regard befitting of their distinct contributions to society, much less their inherent dignity as human beings. The Islamic legal system came to uphold women's rights in ways that no man-made legal system had done up until then. Even beyond the expansive default rights, Islamic law guarantees access to special benefits

---

[1] The Holy Quran. Chapter 33 [The Parties; Arabic: *Al-Ahzab*]. Verse 59.

when stipulated as terms in a binding contract. This means that the present and future for women in Islam carry the potential for an expansion of benefits to be stipulated. Women, especially in past civilizations, had been living in a wretched state with barely any, if any, recognized rights. Women would not come close to the status of men in these societies. Even those civilizations that chant the mantras of enfranchisement and women's rights did not give them their due rights. Women in the west, up until very recently, did not have the status, position, and respect that Islam honored. Due to the errors inherent in manmade legal systems, women were often in flux in a world of changing laws as lawmakers grappled with the issues of legislation and the changing needs of the times. Islam, on the other hand, put in place a set of divine laws that would give women their rights and honor their status, and that can and should be implemented at all times.

God Almighty regards both men and women as members of the faithful community who have a responsibility to one another. All believers in the community must focus on devotion to God. In one verse, God says,

> *But the faithful, men and women, are [guardians] of one another: they bid what is right and forbid what is wrong and maintain the prayer, give the zakat, and obey God and His Apostle. It is they to whom God will soon grant His mercy. Indeed God is all-mighty, all-wise.*[2]

As a society in devotion to God, both men and women guard one another from straying from God's way. Regard-

---

[2] The Holy Quran. Chapter 9 [The Repentance; Arabic: *Al-Tawba*]. Verse 71.

less of gender, all are to act out of devotion to God and uphold their responsibility.

Another verse reveals to us the extent of rewards that each of the two genders will receive. *"Then their Lord answered them, 'I do not waste the work of any worker among you, whether male or female; you are all on the same footing...'"*[3] The issue of reward is of great importance, as it can determine one's fate in the Hereafter. The verse tells us that the worker – regardless whether male or female – receives the compensation for his/her work. The potential rewards are not limited by one's gender.

Gender equality in Islam has been espoused over fourteen centuries ago. However, this equality does not overlook the differing natures of males and females. In certain cases, gender has no role to play, such as in spiritual rewards. In other cases, gender may impact the nature of roles and responsibilities for men and women, respectively. In all cases, Islam's guidelines are a manifestation of Divine Justice. Justice does not always mean uniformity in all aspects. Treating the two genders as if they are the same in every way – the concept that is espoused by some Westerners nowadays – is not fair. There are differences between the two genders that may at times entail different rights, roles and responsibilities. Treating the two genders as if they are the same in all areas is a form of oppression. This places an undue burden on women. For these Western societies that call for equality are placing the burdens of child rearing, maintaining the home, as well as obtaining the necessities of life on women. This should not be expected of man or woman to take on

---

[3] The Holy Quran. Chapter 3 [Arabic: *Aal Imran*]. Verse 195.

alone. Moreover, claims that women should have the same freedom as men, in terms of dress code for instance, have led to women being exploited inappropriately for advertising. In such societies, women in many cases have become judged based more so on their appearance than on the basis of their intellectual merit. Women have been shortchanged in such Western societies and have been made to bear more than their share of responsibility. This has in turn reflected negatively on families, leading to social ailment. Naturally, most women are not superwomen and most men are not supermen. A typical woman has a set of qualities that suit her best for certain rights, responsibilities and roles. A typical man has a different set of qualities that suit him best for certain rights, responsibilities and roles. The two share many qualities, and thus expectedly share various rights, responsibilities and roles. But they also differ, and thus it is expected that their rights, responsibilities and roles should differ accordingly. God Almighty's law for humanity takes all factors into account and should always be understood as a manifestation of Divine Wisdom and Justice.

Yet, there are those who blame Islam for the ill treatment of women. They cite a number of Islamic laws that restrict a woman's dress code in certain situations, such as the concept of *hijab*. They also cite a number of laws that otherwise limit a woman's freedom, such as the fact that the husband has been delegated with the responsibility of guarding his wife and his permission is required before she leaves the home. Of course, the woman is allowed to stipulate that the man grant her this permanently through an irrevocable power of attorney in the marriage contract, or any other binding contract after marriage for that matter.[4] Regardless, we cannot, in this brief section, answer all the questions and concerns in this regard. Rather, we will attempt to shed light on two important issues: (1) modesty and *hijab*, and (2) women at the workplace.

But before we address these two issues, we must first point out that this negative image of Islam has three major causes:

1. The negative role that Western media has played in portraying Islam, where they present only fragments of Islam rather than providing a complete and holistic view. They emphasize only one part of the concept that seems to them reprehensible without considering all the other aspects of the concept and all the other concepts that play on, accentuate, and complete one another. They focus on the issue of *hijab* and condemn it without looking at Islam's rationale for it, or the many laws that give women a high status in this world and the next and that require respect and devotion for women as mothers, wives, and daughters, for example.
2. The negative image that some Muslims have given Islam due to their own malpractices in dealing with women. We see that some Muslims deal with women based on non-Islamic cultural baggage and backward traditions that date back to pre-Islamic times. Whenever a group of people would accept Islam, many a time they kept their customs with them – the good and the bad. While Islamic culture is enriched by the noble traditions and customs of differ-

---

[4] See: Q&A section on the official website of Grand Ayatollah Sistani.

ent Muslims so long as they do not violate Islamic teachings, unjust customs cannot possibly be regarded as part of the religion of Islam. Still, it is painful to see the degree of backwardness that some Muslims live in and that reflects negatively on their great religion. Instead of practicing the high morals of Islam, we see that Muslims fall back into these regressive customs and portray Islam as a backwards religion.

3. The erroneous and fallacious understanding of some Muslims about their faith. Some people pick and choose what to follow of the religion based on their own desires and they interpret its teachings as it suits them best.

*Do you believe in part of the Book and deny another part? So what is the requital of those of you who do that except disgrace in the life of this world? And on the Day of Resurrection, they shall be consigned to the severest punishment. And God is not oblivious of what you do.*[5]

These modes of interpreting Islam have given others such a terrible impression of our faith.

## Modesty and Hijab

God has given the modesty and *hijab* of a woman much care and significance. Islam's focus on the significance of a woman's character and presentation in society by shedding light on Islam's high regard for a woman's role in this life.

---

[5] The Holy Quran. Chapter 2 [Arabic: *Al-Baqara*]. Verse 85.

Islam sees men and women as two complementary and compatible halves of humanity. God says,

> O mankind! Indeed, We created you from a male and a female, and made you nations and tribes that you may identify yourselves with one another. Indeed the noblest of you in the sight of God is the most God-wary among you. Indeed God is all-knowing, all-aware.[6]

As one of the great scholars and philosophers interprets it:

> [Islam views the human race as comprising] of two humans – male and female – and there is no precedence for one over the other except through [each individual's] piety... So [God] made every human a derivation and composition of two humans [i.e. parents], a male and a female, and they are together and in unison the material of [a human's] creation and existence....[7]

Because women constitute an integral part of mankind's existence, upbringing and subsistence, they are to be respected, safeguarded, and protected. Honoring and safeguarding women can foster an environment of purity and morality, allowing humanity to flourish without the social ills that limit individual and societal potential. Divine Wisdom made sure that Islam would institute a number of practices that help guarantee that goal. Islam teaches people to view women, among many other noble qualities, as the vessels of purity that carry humanity. They are the source of sustenance for the infants. They are the foundation that we build our families on, and the warm refuge that nurtures us.

---

[6] The Holy Quran. Chapter 49 [Arabic: *Al-Hujurat*]. Verse 13.
[7] Al-Tabatabaei, *Al-Mizan*, 2:269.

They are the source of education and morality for our youth. Mothers have a status that no man can attain. Their role in the life and upbringing of every individual is generally unmatched.

In honoring and safeguarding women, Islam has instituted the following practices.

*Hijab*

Islam puts a great emphasis on the *hijab* and modesty of a woman and that she, like a man, should also distance herself from all environments of immorality. While both men and women are expected to be modest, the manifestation of modesty differs depending on the nature of each gender, for instance. Similarly, while both men and women have a certain dress code to abide by, each gender's dress code differs due to the differing nature of each gender and the dynamic of interaction between the genders, for example. A woman is like a gem that is to be valued dearly, guarded appropriately in suitable conditions and reserved for the access of only those authorized by God Almighty. When Islam prescribes the *hijab* as the dress code for women outside of the home, it fosters an appearance that commands the respect for her as an individual of intellect and moral character. It deflects the focus from a woman's physical attractiveness as an object of pleasing the debasing desires of the opposite gender. Instead, especially when the women observes Islamic etiquettes in her behavior as well, the *hijab*-wearing woman interacts with society as an elegant individual, beautiful spirit and notable intellect ready to make effective contributions to the advancement of humanity.

Naturally, men are attracted to women. This attraction among husband and wife is beautiful. In general, this attraction allows for the continuation of the human race. However, in both liberal and conservative societies, this attraction is often perverted and used as a drive to subjugate or exploit women to satisfy men's debasing desires. That is why God commands the Prophet (s) to ask the believing women to observe the *hijab* (an Arabic word referring to the Islamic dress code for women, including the veil). God also commands both men and women to lower their gaze and not look at one another lustfully. These are multiple layers of protection for both men and women. By observing these lines of spiritual defense, those who are spiritually ill will be much less likely to harm society overall, and women specifically. Thus, women – the gems of society – are better guarded and honored through the veil of modesty.

The verse of the Quran refers to the *hijab* dress code prescribed by God, not the incomplete, tight, or decorative imitation of the veil wardrobe that has itself become a source of negative attention for debasing desires. As for the proper *hijab*, it is a line of spiritual defense safeguarding women and men alike. The prescribed *hijab* presents women in society as fellow human beings with character and intellect, not as objects to be gazed at or exploited inappropriately. Therefore, the purpose of the veil wardrobe is not to subjugate women to men, but to protect women and men from subjugation – whether that subjugation is subtle or explicit. When women are preyed on by the inappropriate gazes of men in public, this is a form of subjugation. If it is not outright subjugation by men, it is subjugation by Satan and his accomplices, luring people into sin against God Almighty. When women are used as tools of advertisement for the attractiveness of their physical features, this is a form of subjugation. When women are not honored first and foremost for their qualifications in intellect and character, there is subjugation and injustice taking place. The proper *hijab*, in addition to the etiquettes prescribed by Islam, helps protect women and men alike from the deceptions and tricks of Satan and his accomplices. God's prescriptions for humanity, the *hijab* being only one example, safeguards society and help keep individuals on the path toward excellence in this world and the Hereafter.

*Marriage*

Islam also puts great emphasis on the issue of marriage, even early marriage. Whenever there are two suitable and compatible potential spouses, Islam encourages that the two complete one another with God's blessings through a marital bond. Marriage can foster the expression of love between husband and wife, filling that emotional need in their lives. It can also nurture compassion for one another, even when the fire of love is not ablaze. Furthermore, whether young or elderly, marriage can be one of the best means to channel a man and a woman's energies healthily, helping each of them concentrate on moving society forward.

In Islam, marriage is a bond based on compatibility by which a husband and a wife complement one another and generally live their lives together as a family unit. Through marriage, the harmony, continuation and advancement of the human race is safeguarded. One of the major benefits of marriage is that it helps provide an upright childrearing environment. In light of the various benefits and dimensions to marriage, the marital laws and etiquettes in Islam do not only focus on the financial aspects of the marriage such as the bridal gift, inheritance, and other monetary obligations. Rather, the laws and etiquettes also focus on the relationship between the spouses, childrearing, and similar issues. Many of these rules and etiquettes safeguard the rights and roles of the wife in particular. Furthermore, the potential spouse is also able to stipulate some additional benefits in the marriage contract or in any post-marital binding contract. These rights, responsibilities, and Islamic etiquettes uphold the honorable status of women in marriage while guarding their purity and dignity.

*Women in the Public Eye*

Both man and woman are responsible for their appearance in public. As a Muslim, each individual is held to a standard of following God Almighty's prescription for physical, spiritual and intellectual excellence. Moreover, women in Islam have been privileged to some default distinctions that men do not generally enjoy. For instance, the distinct dress code represented in the *hijab* is in many cases recognized as a flag of Islam. A practicing Muslim woman in the public eye is quickly recognized as an ambassador of her faith. Furthermore, Islam requires that a Muslim husband provide his wife with a suitable residence, far from any sources of bother and harm. It is the wife's right that the husband provide for all of her financial needs. She is not required to do any household chores. In certain cases, the husband may be required to hire a maid to serve her. The wife is exempt from many duties outside of the home that men are required to perform. For example, even when the Friday Prayer at the mosque is an obligation for men, it is not required of women. Women are generally allowed to stay at home and consider their homes to be their mosque. These privileges and default responsibilities of the woman to her household have the impact of safeguarding women from the general public eye. Only a select few should have access to the queen. Another dimension to this may be to emphasize the importance of a woman's role in childrearing and building the next generation. This is a fundamental role and serves humanity as a whole. Granted, it is true that the woman's default responsibilities to her household can be otherwise managed or agreed upon, before marriage or after, through stipulations in a binding contract for example. However, there is surely wisdom in why the default rights and responsibilities are the default to begin with.

## Women in the Workplace

Islam does not have a negative view towards women in the workplace, just as it does not have a negative view towards men in the workplace. If, however, being in the workplace entails falling into sins – whether the worker be a man or a woman – then Islam has a problem with that. A person's relationship with God is above all other considerations. There are a number of issues that Islam addresses regarding women in the workplace. All in all, Islam takes a holistic view on the matter that is largely based on the substantive circumstances of the individual woman, as well as social factors surrounding her.

## A Neutral View

There are a number of things that may allow us to deduce that Islam looks at the issue of women in the workplace with a gender neutral lens. Among them are:

1. The marriage of the Grand Prophet (s) and the Mother of the Believers Lady Khadija (a), a woman known as a successful merchant. She owned a wide trade network and the Prophet (s) worked with her on trade for some time. If this was a discouraged or dishonorable thing, the Prophet (s) would have made that clear.

2. There were a number of women at the time of the Prophet (s) that would engage in trade. For example, a woman by the name of Alhawlaa used to sell perfumes to the wives of the Prophet (s), and the Prophet (s) would buy from her. Yet we do not find any religious texts that disparage this. Rather, we see that the Prophet (s) advises Alhawlaa to perfect her trade and never turn to exploitation in her work.

3. Islamic laws permit women to work and engage in trade. They make whatever she earns solely her property independent of her husband's. No matter how much she earns, it remains the responsibility of the husband to supply her with all her necessities. She is not obligated to spend any of her money to support her husband or her family.

4. There are a number of professions that must generally be left for women, as men cannot adequately fulfill them. This includes women's healthcare, nursing, education, and similar professions that rely on

the emotional and childrearing capabilities of the woman.

All of these are indications that Islam looks positively at women in the workplace, or with neutrality to say the least. From these points, we may even infer the importance for a woman to join the work force and not to stifle her abilities in contributing to the community economically and intellectually.

*Discouragement*

On the other hand there are a number of points which allude to discouraging women from entering the labor market. They include:

1. The fact that a man holds the obligation of securing all the necessities of his dependents, including his wife – food, clothing, habitation, etc. This means that a woman's livelihood is secured by her husband, father, or son, and thus does not need to seek her own livelihood. This may indicate that God does not want women to suffer from need and toil for her own livelihood.

2. The many narrations that stress on the importance of the women's role in her home and that the home is her headquarters. The narrations emphasize that a woman should dedicate her time for the rearing of children and for supporting the husband, and made these amongst the best acts that she can perform. It is narrated that the Prophet (s) said, "*Whenever a woman lifts something in the house and places it somewhere*

*else, seeking good in that action, God will look unto her. Whomever God looks unto, He will not punish."*[8]

3. The many narrations that speak of chastity and modesty for a women conflict with a woman's entry into the labor market and being preyed on by the inappropriate gazes of men.
4. A woman holding a job will without a doubt have a negative impact on the family. She will have less time to spend with the husband and the children. When childrearing is given up and made the role of sitters and nannies, that action will have a negative effect on the child and the family. This is in addition to the fact that societies —even modern Western societies – place on the shoulders of the woman the obligation of maintaining the home; all of which creates undue stress and gives the woman a larger share of responsibility than the man.

*Reconciling the Two Views*

We can reconcile the two sets of points as follows.

Firstly, it is permissible for a woman to seek a job and a career. There is no religious text prohibiting that. However, when doing so, she should, as should a man in the workplace, observe the guidelines prescribed by God.

Secondly, when it is unnecessary for a woman to work, it is best for her to remain home, be guarded from unneeded exposure to the spiritually ill men of society, and focus on the wellbeing of her household. Surely, God would love to see a woman dedicated to her family.

---

[8] Al-Tusi, *Al-Amali*, 618.

Islam recognizes the distinct physiological and psychological features of each gender. Accordingly, Islamic law wisely sets rules and regulations for the dynamic of interaction among the genders. Furthermore, Islam encourages a set of recommendations and etiquettes to be observed whenever necessity does not dictate otherwise. The slogan of "Gender Equality" is meaningful so long as it falls within the absolute wisdom of God's prescription for humanity. But the moment that such "equality" becomes unfair and unwise, that is when the slogan is merely a slogan – one void of true merit. God Almighty wants the best for each gender and for every member of human society. Islamic laws and etiquettes help make sure that each gender compliments the other, completes the other, and is safeguarded from unhealthy interaction with the other – all for the advancement of every individual and humanity as a whole.

# TRADE

*In the Name of God the Beneficent the Merciful*

*O mankind! Eat of what is lawful and pure in the earth, and do not follow in Satan's steps. Indeed, he is your manifest enemy.*[1]

Generally, everything God created in this world is at the disposal of mankind, including the Earth that bears fruit and carries livestock. Everything was placed at the service of mankind during his journey towards God. God has allowed us to make use of these blessings and has encouraged us to work to achieve them. He wants us to seek true success and happiness in this world and the next. Of course, all of this becomes possible by following His prescription, the framework of His laws and guidelines.

It's wrong to think that God wants us to live in a state of poverty and need for others. To the contrary, the Quran and the traditions encourage us to make use of the blessings of this world within the boundaries set by God in order to enjoy the best of this world and the next. The Quran states,

---

[1] The Holy Quran. Chapter 2 [The Cow; Arabic: *Al-Baqara*]. Verse 168.

*Say, 'Who has forbidden the adornment of God which He has brought forth for His servants, and the good things of [His] provision?' Say, 'These are for the faithful in the life of this world, and exclusively for them on the Day of Resurrection.' Thus do We elaborate the signs for a people who have knowledge.*[2]

It is also narrated that the Prophet (s) said, "*Surely, God loves to see whenever he blesses a servant the marks of that blessing [and joy] on him, and He abhors misery and discontentment.*"[3] In another narration, Imam Sadiq (a) says, "*The Commander of the Faithful (a) said, 'God is beautiful and loves beauty. And He loves to see the marks of His blessings on His servant.*"[4]

It is clear that God wants us to benefit from all the bounties that He has created for us in this world. In fact, the narrations tell us that these blessings are better fit for the pious because the pious one shows his gratitude to the Creator. Therefore, God is pleased when His righteous servants benefit from His blessings.

## ISLAM AND TRADE

When we look at the narrations of the Prophet (s) and his Holy Family (a), we see them constantly encouraging their followers to engage in trade. It is narrated that the Prophet (s) said, "*Worship is of seventy parts, the best of them is seeking an honest living.*"[5] It is also narrated that Imam Baqir (a) said, "*Surely, I abhor for men to be lazy in regards to the matters of their*

---

[2] The Holy Quran. Chapter 7 [The Heights; Arabic: *Al-A'raf*]. Verse 32.
[3] Al-Harrani, *Tuhaf Al-'Oqool*, 56.
[4] Al-Kulayni, *Al-Kafi*, 6:438.
[5] Ibid, 5:78.

*worldly lives. Whoever is lazy regarding the matters of his worldly life is lazier when it comes to matters of his otherworldly life.*"[6]

There are other narrations that encourage believers to perfect their trade and seek an honest living. Seeking an honest livelihood has a great effect on the person's spirituality and faith.

### Trade as a Form of Worship

One of the reasons for elevating this mode of earning a livelihood over others may be because of the role it plays in strengthening the individual's faith and trust in God. A person who is employed with a set salary will not have that same spiritual effect that being a merchant or entrepreneur brings. Because a merchant or entrepreneur does not have a reliable and consistent source of income, he will more likely feel the need to put his faith and trust in God and continuously beseech him for sustenance.

Of course, not all people will realize this effect, as some may not even think of God in their trade. We are speaking here about the believers who seek closeness to God by all means. For such an individual, engagement in trade can bring him closer to God through the buildup of faith and trust in Him, gratefulness when He bestows His blessings and sustenance, and patience when encountering a loss. There are also a number of ethical characteristics that can be honed through trade. Perhaps that is why trade is emphasized and considered an act of worship. The Prophet (s)

---

[6] Ibid, 5:85.

is reported to have said, *"Worship is ten parts, nine of them are [in] seeking a Halal living."*⁷

If we contemplate on this narration, we will notice that the Prophet (s) restricted seeking a living to one which is *Halal* – an honest living consistent with the teachings of Islam. While we are encouraged to earn a living, everything must be within the guidelines of faith and morals. We are not told to seek wealth for its own sake, but rather to seek an honest living. It's the latter, and not the former, that is considered an act of worship.

*Trade and Honor*

One of the issues that is greatly emphasized by Islam is the issue of decency and honor. A believer's sincere faith and devotion to decency is so honorable in the eyes of God Almighty that God recognizes the honor of the faithful in the holy Quran. God says, *"They say, 'When we return to the city, the [honorable] will surely expel the [abject] from it.' Yet all [honor] belongs to God and His Apostle and the faithful, but the hypocrites do not know."*⁸

In the narration reported from Imam Sadiq (a), he emphasizes the importance of never neglecting honor and decency. He said,

> *God empowered the believers in everything, except that they become abject. Have you not heard God's words,* "Yet all [honor] belongs to God and His Apostle and the faithful"? *The believer will always be honorable and will not be abject. A believer is more honorable than a moun-*

---

⁷ Al-Majlisi, *Bihar Al-Anwar*, 100:9.
⁸ The Holy Quran. Chapter 63 [The Hypocrites; Arabic: *Al-Munafiqoon*]. Verse 8.

*tain. A mountain can be chipped away with pickaxes, but a believer's faith cannot be chipped away.*[9]

Trade and entrepreneurship gives the individual opportunity to be honorable amongst people. Al-Mo'alla ibn Khonays narrates the following, "[Imam Sadiq (a)] saw me one day and I was late to the [my shop in] the market. He said to me *'hurry to your honor.'*"[10] The Imam told him to go and seek out the reason for his honor. A believer must seek this kind of honor because the divine legislator commanded him to do so, and not because of conceit or vainglory. Such vices drive the individual farther from the pleasure of God.

## Trade and the Intellect

It is evident from the narrations that trade plays a large role in developing the intellect and sound judgment. These are things that God wants us to acquire, at the very least for their benefit in securing an honest living in this world. It is narrated that a man told Imam Sadiq (a) that he is doing well financially and that he wants to leave his trade and retire. The Imam (a) replied, *"If you do, your intellectual abilities will decrease."*[11] And there are many similar narrations.

## ISLAM'S INTEREST IN AN HONEST LIVING

The blessings and effects of engaging in a trade are many and we cannot list and explain them all here. What is most important is to note that Islam, with all this emphasis on trade, places boundaries and guidelines for anyone pursuing

---

[9] Al-Kulayni, Al-Kafi, 5:63.
[10] Al-Sadouq, *Man La Yahdaruh Al-Faqih*, 3:192.
[11] Al-Kulayni, *Al-Kafi*, 5:148.

this. Islam requires that the living earned by anyone be *Halal*, a spiritually healthy, honest living. That is why the Quran explicitly states that God has permitted good pleasures and prohibited regressive pleasures. God has commanded that we endeavor to earn a living on this Earth within the boundaries that He has set. Besides, those boundaries are for our own benefit in this world and the Hereafter. God Almighty neither gains any benefit from our obedience nor any harm from our disobedience.

That is why the narrations emphasize that a person must learn the rulings of the religion so that he can pursue an honest living and refrain from any corrupt practices. It is narrated that Imam Ali (a) said,

> *Oh merchants! Learn [the rulings of the faith] before you trade. Learn before you trade. By God, usury crawls through this nation more silently than the crawl of an ant over a smooth rock. Safeguard your wealth with charity. A merchant is [sinful] and the [sinful] are [punished] in hellfire, [that is every merchant] except [the merchant] who takes [only] what is right and gives what is right.*[12]

It is also reported that Imam Sadiq (a) said,

> *Whoever wishes to pursue trade let him seek knowledge of his religion, so that he can come to know what is permissible for him and what is not. Whoever does not learn his religion and trades regardless will be embroiled in doubtful situations [regarding his transactions and wealth, where they are possibly Haram].*[13]

---

[12] Al-Sadouq, *Man La Yahdaruh Al-Faqih*, 3:194.
[13] Al-Mufeed, *Al-Moqni'a*, 591.

Islam does not call its followers to accumulate wealth for wealth's sake. Rather, Islam's concern is with how an individual can rightfully earn an honest living. It's concerned with preventing the individual from pursuing a dishonest living or engaging in usurious transactions, as this all will have a negative effect on the individual's body and soul. *"Those who exact usury will not stand but like one deranged by the Devil's touch. That is because they say, 'Trade is just like usury.' While God has allowed trade and forbidden usury."*[14] This is in addition to the host of negative material and spiritual consequences that this would have on the person and the overall community. Many of the world's problems today may be attributed to dishonorable ways of acquiring wealth, driven by and fostering greed, exploitation, and other social ills.

Of course, it should be clear that Islam's focus on having the individual earn a decent and honest living and to refrain from forbidden practices is all based on the best interest of the individual. Islam acts as a barrier against all that will pollute and corrupt its followers, on all levels – physical, spiritual and intellectual.

God has guaranteed for each individual his sustenance, such that even if everyone in the world conspired to rid him of his sustenance, to override God's system, God will deliver it to him regardless. Thus, sustenance is a blessing granted by God. Granted, God has created a system where our choices and pursuit of God's blessings through worldly means as well as spiritual means are part of the equation determining our sustenance. However, since the overall system is designed by and guaranteed by God, there is no use in fretting

---

[14] The Holy Quran. Chapter 2 [The Cow; Arabic: *Al-Baqara*]. Verse 275.

and being overwhelmed with anxiety over sustenance. Each person's interest lies in seeking the sustenance according to the guidelines God has provided. As for the overall results, those are a test from God Almighty. One must always remember that whatever the result of the equation, God Almighty is testing us with it. Whether it be wealth or poverty, each is a test calling for a display of our true colors.

There is no honor in collecting money by simply any means at one's disposal. Honor comes from earning wealth while preserving ethics and values. How many evils in the world have become acceptable today because of moral bankruptcy? Usury, for example, has become widely accepted despite its evils. The sale of alcohol, a most degenerate sin, has become the mark of the elites. Is this not true corruption?

Wealth is not a goal in and of itself. It is a means employed on the journey toward achieving happiness. But if wealth becomes a reason for the destruction of values and morals and leads to the regression of humanity, then it is better not pursued. If a person cannot stand up to the harmful temptations of wealth, then poverty is a much nobler path.

## Engaging in the Stock Trade

The world of commerce has produced a type of business that is divided into tiny fractions and freely sold and bought amongst traders. The partners – or the stockholders – in these corporations delegate their right to control the business to a board of directors that maintains operations.

Principally, there is no objection to this type of business relationship. Rather than have a limited number of owners, this allows for a large number of stakeholders in the business transactions. Generally, the problem is not with the business form, but with the potential activities of the business. Some businesses may engage in impermissible activities, and some may be created for an impermissible purpose. Participating in forbidden transactions and endorsing forbidden aims are harmful and thus forbidden in God's law.

According to His Eminence, the late Grand Ayatollah Sayyid Aboulqasim Al-Khoei (r), if the business in question carries out forbidden activity, then it is forbidden to purchase their stocks since this entails taking part in and endorsing the forbidden transactions. This would include banks conducting forbidden interest-based transactions, winemakers, department store chains that sell pork, or any other corporation that carries on impermissible activities. A person engaged in this must abandon all forbidden activity immediately and deal with the profits as detailed by his/her Grand Religious Authority. Moreover, if the corporation was originally engaging in only permissible activities and then later became engaged in impermissible activities, one must also abandon all forbidden activity immediately and deal with the profits as detailed by his/her Grand Religious Authority.

With this ruling in mind, according to Grand Ayatollah Al-Khoei (r), investors are allowed to buy stocks of corporations at the capital subscription stage – where the corporation is raising funds in order to start up and commence business activities – provided that he/she sells them before any potential forbidden activities commence. The purchase of these stocks must also not be a forbidden transaction itself, such as attempting to purchase wine merchandise, for instance. Of course, if even this level of participation entails and endorses forbidden activity then it is not allowed either. For detailed rulings concerning particular situations, one should refer to his/her respective Grand Religious Authority.

As for the opinion of His Eminence Grand Ayatollah Sayyid Ali Al-Sistani, it can be summarized in the following points:

There are three key cases to consider regarding stocks:

First, some corporations do not deal with forbidden merchandise or engage in any impermissible activity, such as those that engage in real estate without any forbidden transactions, or manufacturing (of permissible products, of course), or similar activities. Generally, there is no problem in buying and selling the stocks of these companies.

Second, some corporations deal with forbidden merchandise and engage in certain impermissible activities, investing their money in forbidden areas such as selling wine and other things. Purchasing such stocks, attempting to gain shares in the forbidden merchandise, such as wine, is impermissible. A person engaged in this must abandon all forbidden activity immediately and deal with the profits in the ways detailed in the rulings of His Eminence Grand Ayatollah Sayyid Al-Sistani.

Third, some corporations do not deal with forbidden merchandise but engage in some forbidden interest-based transactions (taking interest from Muslims). Grand Ayatollah Sistani's opinion is that one is allowed to buy shares in this type of corporation, if the purchase itself is not a participation in forbidden activity, and provided that he/she informs the corporation that he/she does not authorize them to use his/her purchased shares in impermissible transactions. It is enough to inform them of this even if the company does not end up honoring his/her directive. As is expected, however, if in certain cases even this level of participation entails and endorses forbidden activity then it is not allowed either.

In cases when maintaining stocks in this type of corporation is permissible according to Grand Ayatollah al-Sistani's rulings, profits that are generated could include some that are generated through permissible activities and others that are generated through impermissible activities. Therefore, when a stockholder in such a corporation receives dividends from it, he/she must refer to the detailed rulings of Grand Ayatollah Sayyid al-Sistani to determine how he/she is required to deal with the acquired wealth.

In light of this all, we must direct the readers' attention that the wisest thing to do may very well be to avoid this type of transaction in order to avoid falling into forbidden activity. With the right intention, the further we distance ourselves from impermissible gains and have piety in our hearts, the more God will bless us with the best of his blessings. As He says,

> *Whoever is wary of God, He shall make for him a way out [of the adversities of the world and the Hereafter] and provide for him from whence he does not count upon. And whoever puts his trust in God, He will suffice him. Indeed God*

*carries through His commands. Certainly, God has ordained a measure [and extent] for everything.*[15]

---

[15] The Holy Quran. Chapter 65 [Divorce; Arabic: *Al-Talaq*]. Verses 2 and 3.

# REMEMBRANCE OF IMAM HUSSAIN (A)

*In the Name of God the Beneficent the Merciful*

*Indeed God has bought from the faithful their souls and their possessions for paradise to be theirs: they fight in the way of God, kill, and are killed. A promise binding upon Him in the Torah and the Evangel and the Quran. And who is truer to his promise than God? So rejoice in the bargain you have made with Him, and that is the great success. [The faithful are] penitent, devout, celebrators of God's praise, wayfarers, who bow [and] prostrate [in prayer], bid what is right and forbid what is wrong, and keep God's bounds—and give good news to the faithful.*[1]

The month of Muharram has a characteristic welcome for commemoration and remembrance. It starts off the Islamic calendar with a season of sadness that rejuvenates the Muslim community with the Saga of the Master of Martyrs, Al-Imam Al-Hussain (a). Every year, during this season, we

---

[1] The Holy Quran. Chapter 9 [The Repentance; Arabic: *Al-Tawba*]. Verses 111-112.

renew our allegiance and loyalty to the Household of the Holy Prophet (s). We remember the tragedies that Ahlulbayt (a) endured. We remember how a nation stood against the grandson of the Prophet – the very same nation that he spent every moment of his life building with honor and generosity and strived to save from hellfire.

Why is so much importance placed on the cause of Al-Husain (a)? Why do his followers come out every year in mourning, crying, and pounding their chests over an event that took place about 1400 years ago? Hasn't enough time passed for this sorrow to pass over? Could there be an acceptable intellectual dimension to this sorrow and mourning? Why mourn for Imam Hussain (a) rather than any of the other Immaculate Imams (a)? Why mourn the martyrdom of Imam Hussain (a) more than the death of the Grand Prophet (s)?

These are many issues that are raised about the mourning of Imam Hussain (a). We will attempt to answer them in the following points.

## Mourning – Passion or Rationale?

When we study the phenomenon of mourning over the martyrdom of Imam Hussain (a) and the tragedy of Karbala, we find a number of unique perspectives not found in any other tragedy.

Firstly, it has become a banner and a symbol for an entire school of thought – the followers of the Holy Household of the Prophet (s). Rather, the mourning of Imam Hussain has become the characteristic that distinguishes them from all other Islamic schools of thought. Shiism has become synonymous with mourning for the tragedy of Karbala. Practicing the rites of mourning for the tragedies of the Grand Prophet (s) and his Household (a) has become synonymous with Shiism. This school of thought has taken buildings across this earth and turned them into places of mourning for this individual and his family. Rather, these places of mourning have come to gather other Muslims and non-Muslims as well, and that can be seen in many different nations.

Secondly, the followers of the Holy Household (a), as with other Islamic schools of thought, differ in their degree of adherence to all facets of the religion. However, we still see that no matter the degree of their piety, the masses of followers of the Holy Household (a) come together in mourning during the commemorations of the tragedy of Imam Hussain (a).

Therefore, we must ask: Is this phenomenon of mourning and sorrow that repeats itself every year due to a passionate and emotional reaction to a tragedy, or does it go beyond the emotional appeal? Is there a deeper and more important issue at stake? Is the phenomenon founded on clear theological roots?

We are certain that the great emotions and passions that surround the martyrdom of Imam Hussain (a), and the mourning of all Muslims and even non-Muslims for his tragedy, are not merely a reactionary emotional issue. We are certain of this because of a simple fact. Mankind reacts emotionally whenever they hear a sad story or watch a tragic film. They will shed a few tears if the emotional response is strong enough. But if they hear that story or watch that film another time, their emotional response will usually be weaker. The more they grow accustomed to the tragedy, the less likely they are to respond emotionally. The emotions may become muted and the person usually grows numb to the tragedy. But this is not true when it comes to the tragedy of Imam Hussain (a). Although the memory of the tragedy is repeated at least on an annual basis, our emotions do not fade.

This is because the issue of Imam Hussain (a) is not a reactive emotional issue. If it was so, we would become numb to it and we would not react to it anymore after listening to the tragedy a few times, just like many other emotional events in life. But the tragedy of Imam Hussain (a) is different. That is why he says, "*I am the one killed [who causes tears to flow]. No believer remembers me without weeping.*"[2]

But if the issue of Imam Hussain (a) is not reactive emotion, what is the secret that allowed it to endure to this day?

The tragedy of Imam Hussain (a) has this impact on people's lives because of its religious dimension. A believer deals with it like all the other rituals and worships dictated by the faith. Religious fervor does not decrease by proper practice, but rather it only increases. If a believer tastes the spiritual pleasure of prayer performed properly, he/she does not grow bored of prayer by its repetition, but rather grows closer to it. The same is true for all worships when performed according to the guidelines prescribed by God Almighty.

---

[2] Ibn Qawlaweih, *Kamil Al-Ziyarat*, 215.

## Remembrance of Imam Hussain (a)

The Immaculate Imams (a) laid great emphasis on the importance of the tragedy of Imam Hussain (a) in their teachings to their followers. This emphasis took hold of their hearts and minds. In the school of thought of the Prophet's (s) Progeny (a), the remembrance of Imam Hussain (a) is a great worship. This remembrance aims to bring the goals of God's prescription for humanity to fruition. Purpose is clarified and remembered through Imam Hussain (a) and his sacrifice. Universal principles are manifested in his noble stand for truth, justice and mercy.

There are many religious texts that highlight the religious nature of mourning in all its forms – whether it be visiting the Imam (a), crying for his tragedy, or observing the other rituals of mourning. It is narrated that Imam Baqir (a) said,

> *[On the day of Ashura…] let the believer mourn Hussain (a) and weep over him. Let him command everyone in the house to weep over him. Let him remember in his home the tragedy [of Imam Hussain (a)] by showing [intense grief] over him. Let the believers meet each other to cry over the tragedy of Hussain (a). I am the guarantor [to guarantee] that God will grant them, if they do so, all of these rewards [of two million pilgrimages, Umrahs, and battles alongside the Messenger of God (s) and the Righteous Imams (a)].*[3]

The emotional response to a tragedy like the tragedy of Imam Hussain (a) is not merely reactionary and emotional. Rather, it is built on a basis of faith and is a cause for the revival of true faith. That is why we deal with it as a living issue of creed, and not as a merely historical event.

---

[3] Ibid, 326.

## WHY IMAM HUSSAIN?

Why has the tragedy of Imam Hussain (a) taken this deep religious dimension, while the tragedies of the Prophet (s) and the rest of his Holy Household (a) have not taken the same dimension?

Some may ridicule us for our passion for the tragedy of Imam Hussain (a). Some even erroneously condemn us thinking that we are elevating Imam Hussain (a) over the Grand Prophet (s). They neglect by such a condemnation the fact that we mourn Imam Hussain (a) because he is the beloved grandson of our Prophet (s).

Our Immaculate Imams (a) have warned us that others will not understand the rituals of Imam Hussain (a). It is narrated that when one of the companions of Imam Sadiq (a) complained that people called him a liar when he told them of the great merits of visiting the grave of Imam Hussain (a), Imam Sadiq (a) replied, *"leave the people be. By God! Surely, God boasts about the visitor of Hussain (a)..."*[4]

It is also narrated that Imam Sadiq (a) said,

> *It has reached me that some people of the city of Kufa and others from its suburbs come to the grave of [Imam Hussain (a)] in the mid of the month of Shaaban. There are among them reciters of the Quran, orators who relate [the tragedy], poets [praising] us, and women who weep for his tragedy... All praise to God for making among people those who come to [visit] us, [describe our virtues], and eulogize for us. [All praise to God for] making our enemies those who condemn*

---

[4] Ibid, 272.

*them for their closeness to us, and others [who] threaten them and decry their deeds.*[5]

People who have mocked the followers of the Holy Household (a) have existed for centuries. They have done so because they do not understand these rituals or because they have chosen to disregard the truth and turn to the dark side. We will point out here a few of the important facets that have made the tragedy of Imam Hussain (a) so central to the beliefs of the Shia.

*Preserving the Religion*

Since the time of the Prophet (s), the Umayyads were constantly attempting to destroy and distort the religion. The Commander of the Faithful (a) warned the Muslim community about this when he said,

> *Beware that the worst mischief I fear for you is the mischief of the Umayyads; it is blind and dark. Its sway is general but its ill effects are for particular people. He who remains clear-sighted in it would be affected by distress, and he who remains blind in it would avoid the distress. By God, you will find the Umayyads to be wicked masters after [my departure]. They are like the old unruly she-camel who bites with its mouth, beats with its fore-legs, kicks with its hind legs, and refuses to be milked. They would remain over you till they would leave among you only those who benefit them or those who do not harm them. Their calamity would continue till you would not be able to win over them except as a slave wins over his master or a follower over his leader.*[6]

---

[5] Ibid, 539. See also: Al-Amili, *Wasael Al-Shia*, 10:468.
[6] Al-Radi, *Nahj Al-Balagha*, 1:183, Sermon 93.

There was a real danger to Islam posed by the Umayyads. None of the Imams (a) had to take such a decisive stance against such a great evil as Imam Hussain (a) did. Therefore, the martyrdom of Imam Hussain (a) and his revolution served to protect Islam against the forces that attempted to destroy and distort its teachings. It allowed the Muslim community to rise up again after a period of hibernation during the reign of Muawiya and Yazid. After the sacrifice of Imam Hussain (a), who would dare mess with the teachings of the religion? Imam Hussain (a) declared his message to the world when he said,

> *I did not come out due to [conceit, nor out of arrogance], nor as a corruptor, nor as an oppressor. I have come out to call for reform in the nation of my grandfather [the Prophet (s)]. I wish to call for what is good, and to forbid what is evil. I wish to walk on the path of my grandfather and my father Ali ibn Abi Talib (a).*[7]

The movement of Imam Hussain (a) was one of reform. It called for a return back to the values that were taught by the Grand Prophet (s). And because there is in every era a group of people that wish to distort religion so that it becomes agreeable to their foolish desires, the movement of Imam Hussain (a) must live on. The memory of this great tragedy must go on so that we remember the reason behind the great sacrifice. We must remember Imam Hussain (a) as long as there are those who wish to distort the religion. The memory of Imam Hussain (a) inspires us to reject anyone who would wish to do distort the guidance God Almighty wants for us.

---

[7] Al-Majlisi, *Bihar Al-Anwar*, 44:329.

## The Rights of the Household of the Prophet

Through the emphasis of the Immaculate Imams (a) on the tragedy of Imam Hussain (a), we understand the great role that the tragedy played in spreading the message of the Holy Household (a). Whenever anyone hears of the tragedy of Imam Hussain (a), his family, and his companions, they come to love this oppressed martyr. When a person comes to know the values of Imam Hussain (a) and begins to take his side, he/she takes the side of truth, justice, guidance, and naturally the Immaculate Imams (a) after Hussain (a). We see that the Holy Household, despite all the restrictions that were imposed on them from the oppressive governments of the time, they would always stress to their followers the importance of keeping the memory of Imam Hussain (a) alive. This memory sheds light on the rights of the holy household of guidance, the guardians of the faith.

## Universal Principles

One of the key reasons for which the tragedy of Imam Hussain (a) became so fundamental to the Shia is that Imam Hussain (a) and his camp manifested Islam in its true light, away from the distortions of the Umayyads and others. The tragedy shows the true humanitarian and divine principles that Islam espouses. Showing conviction regarding these values in times of luxury may be easy for many. But the truly virtuous individual is the one that exhibits these virtues in the most dire of situations. Imam Hussain (a) led a movement of reform to bring the nation back to the divine values of justice and virtue. He did not stray from this even while he faced the most brutal of massacres. Rather, he manifested divine principles through all his actions.

Imam Hussain (a) manifested sincere belief in the One True God through submission to His will and sacrifice for His sake. This is evident in his supplications, as it is narrated that he would say, *"the pleasure of God is our pleasure. We are patient with His tribulations and He compensates us with the rewards of the patient."*[8] He would submit to the will of God even when he sees his most beloved face death at the hands of evil-doers, without a single sign of discontentment or impatience. His movement was a manifestation of patience and submission to the will of God in its purest forms.

Imam Hussain (a) manifested the highest levels of nobility and honor. He rejected at all times to disgracefully concede to the oppressors. He would declare this multiple times throughout his journey. He would say, *"We will never be disgraced"*; *"I will not give you my allegiance in disgrace, and I will not flee from you like a slave"*; and *"Rather, I don't see in death [in this situation] anything other than happiness, and life with these oppressors is nothing but depravity."* These are a few of the eternal words that he uttered during his sacred movement.

Imam Hussain (a) also manifested great moral character throughout his movement. He would be the one to allow the enemy and their horses to drink of the water he controls. Later, the enemy would slaughter him and his family thirsty. He would refuse to be the one to start the battle even though he has been besieged for days. He would still walk up to enemy lines and advise them about the perils of their ways. His heart, filled with the mercy of God, would have wanted the other side to come to their senses and repent to God before it was too late, before the sword would

---

[8] Al-Maghribi, *Sharh Al-Akhbar*, 3:146.

come between them. It is not far-fetched to imagine that Imam Hussain (a) shed tears as he contemplated the other side's awful crimes against God and humanity. They would force him to fight them in defense of all that was holy.

There are many other important dimensions that the movement and tragedy of Imam Hussain (a) exhibit. The emotional, intellectual, and moral dimensions of his movement allowed it to take center stage in the hearts and minds of the followers of the school of thought of the Holy Household (a). It was also that point from which they drew the strength to hold on to their faith, defend their religion, and to propagate it throughout the world.

Reviving the remembrance of Imam Hussain (a) and commemorating his tragedy through the rituals during the Ashura season is an answer to the call of the Immaculate Imams (a). The season of this tragedy is annually observed, allowing us to draw lessons from these noble souls and model our behavior after their example. This is all in honor for those who sacrificed their lives so that Islam can remain alive in its true form, away from all distortions. It remains a declaration of truth in the face of the oppressors throughout the ages and in all generations. It is an embodiment of the concepts of virtue and humanity that we must all live by.

# BIBLIOGRAPHY

## Religious Scripture

The Holy Quran

## Other Sources

Al-Amili, Muhammad ibn Al-Hassan. *Wasael Al-Shia*. Beirut: Daar Ihya Al-Torath Al-Arabi.

Al-Barqi, Ahmad ibn Muhammad. *Al-Mahasin*. Tehran: Daar Al-Kutub Al-Islamiya, 1950.

Al-Bayhaqi, Ahmad ibn Al-Hussein. *Al-Sunan Al-Kubra*. Daar Al-Fikr.

Al-Borojourdi, Agha Hussein. *Jami' Ahadeeth Al-Shia*. Qum: Al-Matba'a Al-Ilmiyya, 1978.

Al-Bukhari, Muhammad ibn Ismael. *Sahih Bukhari*. Beirut: Daar Al-Fikr, 1981.

Al-Daylami, Al-Hassan. *Irshad Al-Qulub*. Qum: Al-Shareef Al-Murtada Press, 1983.

Al-Ghazali, Muhammad ibn Muhammad. *Al-Mustasfa*.

Al-Hakim, Muhammad Baqir. *Daur Ahlulbayt fi Bina al-Jama'a al-Saliha*. Qum: Al-Alami, 1997.

Al-Hakim, Muhammad Taqi. *Al-Usool Al-'Aamma lil Fiqh Al-Muqarin*. Muassasat Aal Al-Bayt, 1979.

Al-Harrani, Al-Hassan ibn Ali. *Tuhaf Al-'Oqool*. Qum: Muasasat Al-Nashr Al-Islami, 1983.

Al-Hilli, Al-Hassan ibn Yusuf. *Minhaj al-Karamah*.

Al-Hindi, Ali Al-Muttaqi. *Kanz Al-'Ummal*. Muasasat Al-Risala, 1989.

Al-Huwayzi, Abd Ali. *Nour Al-Thaqalayn*. Qum: Ismailian.

Al-Ihsaei, Muhammad ibn Ali. *'Awali Al-La'ali*. Qum: Sayyid Al-Shuhada, 1983.

Al-Kulayni, Muhammad ibn Yaqoub. *Al-Kafi*. Tehran: Daar Al-Kutub Al-Islamiya, 1968.

Al-Maghribi, Al-Nu'man ibn Muhammad. *Sharh Al-Akhbar*. Qum: Muassasat Al-Nashr Al-Islami, 1993.

Al-Majlisi, Muhammad Baqir. *Bihar Al-Anwar*. Beirut: Al-Wafaa, 1983.

Al-Majlisi, Muhammad Baqir. *Mir'at al-'uqul fi Sharh Akhbar 'al al-Rasul*. Tehran: Daar Al-Kutub Al-Islamiya, 1983.

Al-Miyanji, Ali Al-Ahmadi. *Mawaqif Al-Shia*. Qum: Muasasat Al-Nashr Al-Islami, 1995.

Al-Mufeed, Muhammad ibn Muhammad. *Al-Moqni'a*. Qum: Muassasat Al-Nashr Al-Islami, 1989.

Al-Nouri, Mirza Hussain. *Mustadrak Al-Wasael*. Beirut: Mu'asasat Aal Al-Bayt li Ihya' Al-Torath.

Al-Radi, Muhammad ibn Al-Hussain. *Nahj Al-Balagha*. Beirut: Daar Al-Ma'rifa.

Al-Reyshahri, Muhammad. *Al-Haj wa al-'Umrah fi al-Kitab wa al-Sunnah*. Daar Al-Hadeeth.

Al-Reyshhari, Muhammad. *Mizan Al-Hikma*. Cairo: Daar Al-Hadith, 1995.

Al-Sadouq, Muhammad ibn Ali. *'Ilal Al-Sharae'*. Najaf: Al-Matbaa Al-Haydaria, 1966.

Al-Sadouq, Muhammad ibn Ali. *'Oyun Akhbar Al-Rida*. Beirut: Al-A'lami, 1984.

Al-Sadouq, Muhammad ibn Ali. *Al-Khisal*. Qum: Jama'at Al-Mudarriseen, 1982.

Al-Sadouq, Muhammad ibn Ali. *Al-Tawheed*. Qum: Jama'at Al-Mudariseen.

Al-Sadouq, Muhammad ibn Ali. *Man La Yahdaruh Al-Faqih*. 2nd ed. Qum: Jama'at Al-Mudarriseen.

Al-Sadr, Muhammad Baqir. *Al-Fatawa Al-Wadhiha*. Beirut: Daar Al-Taaruf, 1983.

Al-Shaheed Al-Thani, Zayn Al-Deen bin Ali Al-Amili. *Munyat Al-Mureed*. Maktab Al-Ilam Al-Islami,1988.

Al-Shirazi, Nasir Makarim. *Al-Amthal*. Madrasat Ameer Al-Mumineen.

Al-Subhani, Jaafar. *Sirat al-A'immah*. Muassasat Al-Imam Al-Sadiq.

Al-Tabari, Muhammad ibn Jareer. *Nawadir Al-Mo'jizat*. Qum: Madrasat Al-Imam Al-Mahdi, 1989.

Al-Tabatabaei, Muhammad Hussain. *Tafsir Al-Mizan*. Qum: Jama'at Al-Mudarriseen.

Al-Tabrasi, Ahmad ibn Ali. *Al-Ihtijaj*. Najaf: Al-Nu'man, 1966.

Al-Tabrasi, Ameen Al-Deen. *Mujamma' Al-Bayan*. Beirut: Al-A'lami, 1995.

Al-Tusi, Muhammad ibn Al-Hassan. *Al-Amaali*. Qum, 1993.

Al-Tusi, Muhammad ibn Al-Hassan. *Misbah Al-Mutahajjid*. Beirut: Fiqh Al-Shia, 1991.

Al-Wasiti, Kafi Al-Deen Al-Laithi. *'Uyoon Al-Hikam wa Al-Mawa'ez*. Qum: Daar Al-Hadith.

Al-Yazdi, Muhammad Kadim. *Al-Urwat Al-Wuthqa*.

Ibn Abi Al-Hadeed Al-Mutazili. *Sharh Nahj Al-Balagha*. Beirut: Daar Ihya Al-Torath Al-Arabi, 1965.

Ibn Hajar, Ahmad. *Al-Sawa'eq Al-Muhriqa*. Istanbul: Maktabat Al-Haqiqa, 2003.

Ibn Qawlaweih, Jaafar ibn Muhammad. *Kamil Al-Ziyarat*. Qum: Muasasat Al-Nashr Al-Islami, 1996.

Ibn Shahrashoob, Muhammad ibn Ali. *Al-Manaqib*. Najaf: Al-Matbaa Al-Haydaria, 1956.

Ibn Tawuus, Ali ibn Moussa. *Iqbaal Al-A'mal*. Qum: Maktab Al-Ilam Al-Islami, 1993.

www.ingramcontent.com/pod-product-compliance
Lightning Source LLC
LaVergne TN
LVHW011416080426
835512LV00005B/98